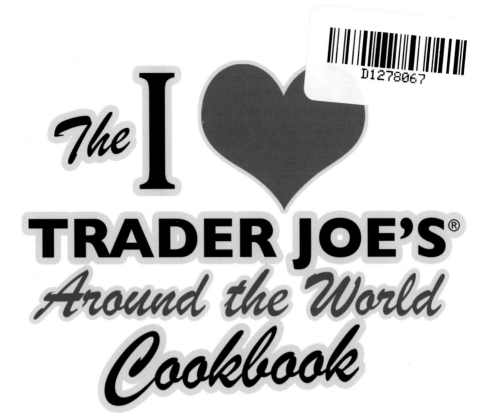

The I ♥ TRADER JOE'S® Around the World Cookbook

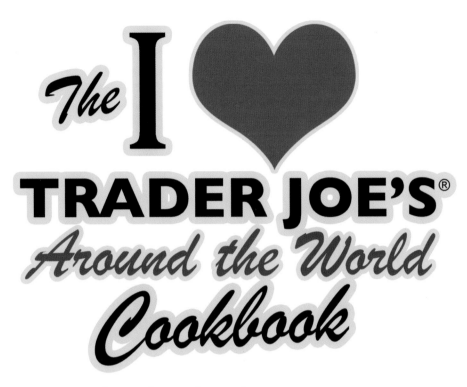

The I ❤ TRADER JOE'S® Around the World Cookbook

More than 140 International Recipes Using Foods from the World's Greatest Grocery Store

Cherie Mercer Twohy

ULYSSES PRESS

Published by
Ulysses Press
P.O. Box 3440
Berkeley, CA 94703
www.ulyssespress.com

ISBN: 978-1-56975-988-2
Library of Congress Catalog Number 2011926026

Printed in Korea by Artin Printing Company through We Think

10 9 8 7 6 5 4 3 2

Acquisitions Editor: Keith Riegert
Managing Editor: Claire Chun
Editors: Lauren Harrison, Leslie Evans
Proofreader: Barbara Schultz
Index: Sayre Van Young
Design: what!design @ whatweb.com
Cover artwork: design elements © ekinsdesigns/istockphoto.com; Old World map © paulojgon/shutterstock. com; Eiffel tower © Jiri Vaclavek/shutterstock.com; bullfighter © Alvaro Cabrera Jimenez/shutterstock. com; Maya calendar © Lukiyanova Natalia / frenta/shutterstock.com; India stamp © RLN/shutterstock. com; bowl of rice © Roxana Bashyrova/shutterstock.com; salsa and guacamole © Judi Swinks Photography; farfalle © Madlen/shutterstock.com; castanets Dover images
Recipes pictured on pages 16, 23, 27, 32, 39, 48, 53, 62, 69, 75, 80, 88, 97, 107, 112, 118, 123, 128, 136, 145, 152, 158, 165, 175, 182 © Judi Swinks Photography
Food stylist for pictured recipes: Anna Hartman-Kenzler
Other interior photos: see page 192

TABLE OF CONTENTS

ACKNOWLEDGMENTS

Writing a cookbook is an exhilarating, fascinating, delicious and occasionally frustrating experience—much like shopping at Trader Joe's! The team at Ulysses Press has guided me through the process three times now, and for this I am very grateful. Lauren Harrison is a painstaking, patient saint of an editor, and I have truly enjoyed working with her on each of the books.

I'm so delighted to be represented by the amazing Lisa Ekus and all the talented folks at the Lisa Ekus Group, and I'm grateful for all the help and support. Can't wait for the next adventure!

I would love to have the chance to personally thank the visionary Joe Coulombe, founder of the Trader Joe's empire, for making shopping such fun. He imbued the company with a brilliant business sense, but also with a fun spirit that's evident whenever you find yourself bobbing down the aisle to a Beach Boys tune. The crews at the many Trader Joe's I've visited over the years have been unfailingly upbeat, friendly, and helpful—can you say that about your big-box shopping experience? TJ's does it right, and I'm very grateful.

My cooking school, Chez Cherie (www.chezcherie.com), has hosted thousands of students over the years, and we're amazed by the warmth and enthusiasm we've experienced from them. Thanks to all of you, and we hope to see you in the kitchen soon! Our staff are culinary rock stars, and we are so very grateful for their support and help. Christine Delgado, GeGe Engwald-Parry, Whitnee Haston, and Valerie Barth—thank you for everything you do so gracefully and supportively. We'd have to lock the doors without you. Anna Ramirez, here's to another happy year in the suds! We're blessed with an amazing cadre of supportive friends, who have been unfailing cheerleaders for the school and these books. They happily devour test recipes, provide feedback and encouragement, and are a generally wonderful bunch. Y'all know who you are—and we love ya! Let's clink wineglasses soon.

My family—well, they are the best! My husband, Steve, is the handyman, muscleman, and host at the cooking school, and keeps everything going so the show can go on each week. I can't believe our kids are all grown up, and I *could not* be prouder of any one of them. Matthew, Kevin, and Brenna, you are my joy and my heart, and the best thing your dad and I ever did! Get your feet back under our table soon!

And finally, to the readers and cooks who have been so supportive of the I Love Trader Joe's cookbooks, sincere thanks for your enjoyment and positive response. You've amazed and overwhelmed me, and I love to know that these recipes are gracing your tables. Nothing could please me more! *Merci*.

⊙ INTRODUCTION

*T*rader Joe's was the first exotic experience in my life. Growing up in Southern California, the local Joe's was a treasure trove of cool and unusual stuff from distant locations. A stroll down the aisles revealed cheeses from Italy, France, and Switzerland, beers from Japan and Belgium, and cookies from just about anywhere. For a kid who'd never been on an airplane, it was quite a heady grocery shopping experience. Even back then, I loved to read the flowery descriptions of the wares and dream of visiting Madrid while munching Manchego. I think part of my wanderlust was inspired by the fascinating items from far-flung places I saw and tasted in those visits to Trader Joe's.

That very idea had inspired TJ's founder Joe Coulombe—his target market was said to be well-educated and well-traveled folks with paychecks smaller than their sophisticated palates. His brilliant concept was to bring some of the flavors that those people may have fallen in love with on their backpacking, "Europe on $5 a day" adventures into his new stores at great prices. Add super wine buys, and a tropical, casual vibe, and a crazy-cool empire was born. Thanks, Mr. C.—I'm your biggest fan.

While the offerings have changed over time, and continue to change (to my deep regret), the variety of products from all over the world continues to fascinate. What a great job those buyers have, traveling the world in search of the best quality and price on chocolates, anchovies, and frozen appetizers. And wine! While I am certain that even *that* job has its downsides, it continues to be on the short list of professions I'd like other than my own if my great job running a cooking school and writing cookbooks ever comes to an end.

Though I absolutely appreciate the company's swing toward locally sourced produce (as well as the shift to individually sold produce items, rather than plastic clamshell packaging—thumbs up on that, TJ's!), I have yet to be pulled into full-time locavore status, nor will I be likely to succumb, with the continuing lure of unctuous soft cheeses and the green-gold array of olive oils from Tuscany and Spain. Although, in my defense, my house olive oil from TJ's is in fact a product of California, as am I!

Given the internationally sourced array of products, an internationally themed Trader Joe's cookbook makes perfect sense. I've had such fun prowling the aisles with regional cuisines in my head, putting together these recipes with the idea of one-stop shopping in mind. While the recipes may not always include strictly authentic ingredients, I've worked hard to bring similar flavors (and tasty ones) to the table, using only ingredients found at Trader Joe's. Let's face facts: There is currently no galangal, garam masala, or fish sauce stocked at TJ's. But with the offerings constantly shifting, any of these might very well show up on a shelf soon! So the recipes in this book represent riffs on the flavors of many locations, and ideas for how to use TJ's ingredients to bring you closer to the cuisines of different countries.

As always, I encourage you to explore, experiment, and expand on these recipes with your own interpretations. As all loyal TJ's shoppers know, you may not find all the items on your shopping list on each visit to the store. Products go in and out of stock, are discontinued, or mysteriously disappear and reappear as suppliers change or reformulate an item's ingredients. We who love TJ's become accustomed to this game. But I can just about guarantee that if one or two things on your list aren't available, you'll find at least that many new intriguing products to fill in the gaps in your shopping basket! Devotion to Trader Joe's requires nimble flexibility, and many of the recipes in this book beg for substitutions. If your store is out of Artichoke and Red Pepper Tapenade, here's your chance to get creative—try another spread, chutney, or condiment in its place. A number of the recipes in this collection are "tried and true" dishes—recipes that also appear in *The I Love Trader Joe's* and *The I Love Trader Joe's Party* books. I've gotten great response on these recipes, and they've become family favorites for readers. I'd love to hear from you if you come up with something great, or if one of these recipes becomes a favorite at your table. Send me an e-mail at cherie@ilovetraderjoes.com.

FRENCH FLAIR

An admitted Francophile, I've probably spent more travel hours in France than any other locale—I've certainly spent more fantasy travel hours there! The days of heavy, sauce-centered, labor-intensive meals are pretty much *passé* in Paris (how do you think those *jeunes filles* stay so thin?). Of course, with Trader Joe as your sous chef, you'll save so much time on prep, you'll have time for *un verre de vin*. From Trader Joe's, *n'est-ce pas*? *Santé*!

POTATO-FENNEL-LEEK SOUP
with SMOKY CHEESE

When the kitchen windows are steamed up from a fragrant pot of soup bubbling on the stovetop, all's right in my world. This one tastes like it simmered all day, although a mere half hour is all it takes to get it on the table.

1 tablespoon butter or olive oil

1 cup fresh or frozen sliced leeks, thawed if frozen

1 bulb fennel, thinly sliced

2 cubes frozen crushed garlic

1½ pounds russet potatoes, peeled and cubed

3 cups vegetable or chicken broth

1 cup Trader Joe's Shredded Smoked Cheese Blend

salt and freshly ground black pepper

VEGETARIAN (IF VEGETABLE STOCK IS USED), GLUTEN-FREE

In a large saucepan, heat the butter or olive oil over medium-high heat. Sauté the leeks and fennel until softened, about 6 minutes. Add the garlic and sauté 1 minute. Add the potatoes and broth. Bring to a boil, reduce the heat to low, and simmer until the potatoes are tender, about 20 minutes. Puree in the pan with an immersion blender. To use a food processor or stand blender, strain the soup, reserving both liquid and solids, and puree the solids, using a little of the liquid; then recombine the puree with the remaining liquid. Return the soup to the saucepan and rewarm over low heat if necessary. Off heat, add the cheese and stir to melt. Season to taste with salt and pepper.

Serves: 4 to 6
Prep Time: 15 minutes
Cooking Time: 40 minutes

FAST *and* FAB FRENCH ONION SOUP

The very sight of a bowl of cheesy-gooey French onion soup makes me nostalgic. No matter where I am when I break through that molten crust, I mentally teleport to that bistro in St. Germain des Près. The aroma of that melted cheese, mingling with the rich beefy soup smell . . . je l'aime!

2 tablespoons butter

2 medium onions, thinly sliced

½ cup red wine

4 cups beef broth

salt and freshly ground black pepper

4 slices artisanal bread, lightly toasted

2 cups Trader Joe's Swiss and Gruyère Shredded Cheese Blend

In a large sauté pan or skillet, heat the butter over medium-low heat. Sauté the onions, stirring frequently, until very soft and golden, 15 to 20 minutes. Increase the heat to high, add the wine, and bring to a boil. Reduce the heat to medium-low and simmer for 5 minutes. Add the beef broth, and season to taste with salt and pepper. Preheat the broiler and set an oven rack about 8 inches from the heating element. Place four ovenproof bowls on a rimmed baking sheet. Divide the onions and liquid among the bowls. Cut the bread slices to fit the bowls, tuck them in on top of the soup, and cover each slice with one-quarter of the cheese. Place under the broiler just until the cheese melts, watching carefully to avoid burning.

Serves: 4

Prep Time: 10 minutes

Cooking Time: 40 minutes

. . . .

For the bread, TJ's Pain Pascal Organic Demi Miche is perfect.

. . . .

SALADE VERTE

This is my go-to salad whenever the main dish has a French accent. You can play around with the ingredients—grapes or figs in place of apples, bacon or no bacon, maybe some chèvre rounds in place of the blue cheese. For the bacon, TJ's Uncured Apple Smoked Bacon is a good choice.

VINAIGRETTE:

salt and freshly ground black pepper

1 tablespoon Dijon mustard

2 tablespoons red wine vinegar

2 tablespoons olive oil

4 tablespoons canola oil

4 strips good-quality bacon, cut into small pieces

½ medium green apple, unpeeled

½ lemon, if cutting up the apple ahead

6 ounces soft-leaf lettuce, such as mâche or butter lettuce, or Trader Joe's Baby Spring Mix

2 ounces Roquefort cheese, crumbled

¼ cup toasted walnuts, coarsely chopped

For the vinaigrette: Put a pinch of salt and the mustard in a small bowl and whisk together. Add the vinegar and whisk. Slowly drizzle in a little of the olive oil, whisking constantly. Continue to add the olive oil and the canola oil as you whisk, until the oil is incorporated and the vinaigrette is slightly thickened. Taste the vinaigrette and adjust the seasoning with salt and pepper. Set aside.

In a medium sauté pan or skillet over medium heat, sauté the bacon pieces until crisp. Drain on paper towels.

To cut the apple into matchsticks, cut it in half, stem to blossom end. Lay the halves, cut sides down, on the cutting board. Cut the apple halves into thin slices, skipping over the core section. Then stack up a few of those slices, and cut into matchsticks. Repeat with the rest of the slices. Do this right before you serve the salad so the apples don't turn brown. If you need to cut them ahead of time, pop the matchsticks into a bowl of water with some lemon juice squeezed in. Drain well before adding to the salad.

To assemble the salad, arrange a bed of lettuce either on a platter or individual plates. Arrange the bacon, Roquefort, apple matchsticks, and walnuts atop the lettuce. Drizzle the vinaigrette lightly over the composed salad.

Serves: 4
Prep Time: 10 minutes
Cooking Time: 5 minutes

CROQUE MONSIEUR

The translation of the sandwich's name is "Mr. Crispy." Gotta love that, and the taste surpasses the cuteness in a big way. Crisp exterior melds with melting, cheesy richness. Oui, s'il vous plaît!

BÉCHAMEL (WHITE SAUCE):

4 tablespoons butter

4 tablespoons flour

¾ cup milk

1 teaspoon Dijon mustard

1 egg yolk, lightly beaten

salt and white pepper

ground nutmeg

1 tablespoon butter

8 slices Trader Joe's Gourmet White Bread, or another good-quality white bread

1 cup shredded Gruyère cheese (4 ounces)

4 slices good-quality ham (Black Forest or Rosemary Ham)

VEGETARIAN (IF YOU OMIT THE HAM)

For the béchamel: In a small saucepan over medium heat, melt the butter and whisk in the flour. Cook until the mixture is smooth and smells nutty, 2 to 3 minutes. Add the milk and bring to a boil. Reduce the heat to medium-low and simmer until thickened, about 4 minutes. Stir in the mustard. Add about one-quarter of the hot milk mixture to the egg yolk, stirring as you add. When the mixture is well blended, return it to the remainder of the hot milk. Season to taste with salt, white pepper, and a little nutmeg.

Preheat the broiler. Butter one side of each slice of bread. Place the slices, butter side down, on a work surface, and spread the plain sides with about 1 tablespoon of the sauce. Sprinkle about 2 tablespoons Gruyère on half the bread slices. (Reserve a little cheese for the tops of the sandwiches.) Top the cheese with a slice of ham, then top with one of the remaining bread slices with the buttered side out. Heat a sauté pan or skillet and brown the sandwiches on each side. Spread a little white sauce on the top of each sandwich, and sprinkle with the remaining cheese. Place the sandwiches under the broiler, watching carefully, until the tops are browned and bubbly, just 1 to 2 minutes.

Serves: 4
Prep Time: 15 minutes
Cooking Time: 20 minutes

TARTE FLAMBÉE

This Alsatian specialty is also known as flammekueche. *Whatever you call it, it's decadent and so satisfying. A tiny slice will generally suffice. (But a second can't hurt, right?)*

4 strips bacon, chopped

1 medium red onion, thinly sliced

salt and freshly ground black pepper

½ cup ricotta cheese

½ cup crème fraîche

1 tablespoon flour

1 sheet frozen Trader Joe's Artisan Puff Pastry, thawed, but kept cold

thyme sprigs, for garnish (optional)

Preheat the oven to 425°F and line a rimmed baking sheet with parchment paper. In a medium sauté pan or skillet over medium-high heat, cook the bacon until it is just beginning to crisp, 3 to 5 minutes. Transfer the bacon with a slotted spoon to a paper towel, and let drain. Add the onion to the pan, and sauté until tender, about 10 minutes. Season lightly with salt and pepper. Transfer with a slotted spoon to a plate, and let cool to room temperature. In a medium bowl, stir together the ricotta, crème fraîche, and flour. Season lightly with salt and pepper. Place the puff pastry on the prepared baking sheet. Spread the ricotta mixture evenly over the pastry, leaving a 1-inch border on all sides. Evenly scatter the onions over the surface and garnish with the bacon. Bake until the pastry is crisp, 15 to 18 minutes. Garnish with thyme sprigs, if using.

Serves: 2 to 4

Prep Time: 10 minutes

Cooking Time: 45 minutes

• •

Puff pastry is carried seasonally at TJ's, so grab a couple to stick in the freezer so you can whip up a tart any time of year. TJ's carries a frozen version of this great treat, labeled Tarte d'Alsace. It says it "serves 4," but some days I don't even know three people I'd share it with. Does that make me a bad person?

• •

POTATO GRATIN *with* GOAT CHEESE

This technique of starting the gratin on top of the stove, instead of doing it all in the oven, cooks the potatoes in far less time than the traditional method.

3 pounds russet potatoes, peeled and thinly sliced

2 to 3 cups chicken or vegetable broth, or half broth and half milk

salt and Trader Joe's Rainbow Pepper Blend pepper

4 ounces goat cheese

1 teaspoon dried thyme

VEGETARIAN (IF VEGETABLE BROTH IS USED), GLUTEN-FREE (IF ALL BROTH IS USED)

Preheat the oven to 400°F. In a large sauté pan or skillet, pour a little of the broth, then add the potatoes. Add enough broth just to cover. Season with salt and pepper, and bring the liquid to a boil over medium heat. Reduce the heat to medium-low and simmer, stirring to separate the potato slices. Simmer until the potato slices are nearly tender, but not falling apart, 10 to 12 minutes. In a 9 x 13-inch ovenproof casserole dish, layer half the potatoes. Crumble half the goat cheese on top, and sprinkle on half the thyme. Repeat with the remaining potatoes, goat cheese, and thyme. Pour any remaining sauce from the pan into the dish. Bake until the potatoes are tender, about 30 minutes. Remove from the oven and let stand for 10 minutes to complete cooking and allow the sauce to be absorbed before serving.

Serves: 4 to 6
Prep Time: 15 minutes
Cooking Time: 45 minutes

CHAMPAGNE CHICKEN *with* CHAMPIGNONS

Simple enough for a weeknight, elegant enough for company, this chicken dish is rich and flavorful. Serve over rice or pasta, with haricots verts (French green beans) or roasted asparagus.

1 tablespoon butter

1½ pounds boneless, skinless chicken breasts or thighs, or a combination

2 cubes frozen crushed garlic

2 shallots, thinly sliced

6 ounces white or crimini mushrooms, thinly sliced

¾ cup Champagne or sparkling wine

salt and white pepper

½ to ¾ cup heavy cream

GLUTEN-FREE

In a large sauté pan or skillet, heat the butter over medium heat. Sauté the chicken until no longer pink on the outside, about 4 minutes on each side. Add the garlic and shallots to the pan, and sauté until the shallots are softened, about 4 minutes. Add the mushrooms and Champagne or sparkling wine (it will fizz up, then subside) and season lightly with salt and white pepper. Cover the pan and simmer, turning the chicken once, until cooked through, 10 to 15 minutes. Transfer the chicken to a warm platter. Increase the heat to high and reduce the cooking liquid until about ¼ cup remains, about 2 to 3 minutes. Add the cream and reduce by half, about 4 minutes. Pour the sauce over the chicken on the platter and serve.

Serves: 4
Prep Time: 10 minutes
Cooking Time: 30 minutes

SOUTH OF FRANCE HALIBUT

Recipes don't get much easier than this one, but the payoff is big Provençal deliciousness. Simple and fast, but don't let that fool you. This one's a keeper.

1 (13.4-ounce) jar Trader Joe's Ratatouille

2 cubes frozen crushed garlic

½ cup dry white wine

1 pound wild halibut, frozen or thawed

salt and freshly ground black pepper

red chile pepper flakes

In a medium sauté pan or skillet over medium-high heat, combine the ratatouille, garlic, and white wine and bring to a simmer. Add the fish and simmer until a knife blade inserted into the center comes out warm to the touch, about 6 minutes for thawed fish, 20 minutes for frozen. Season to taste with salt, pepper, and chile pepper flakes.

Serves: 4

Prep Time: 5 minutes

Cooking Time: less than 10 minutes for thawed fish, about 20 minutes for frozen

COQUETTE AU VIN

Coq au vin is the famous French dish using red wine and a rooster. Back in the day, my mom used to make a version of it we called "purple chicken." I've changed up her rendition to be a little lighter, more feminine, maybe. Also, I don't know if the chickens I'm using are hens or roosters, but I hope the dish is coquettish, in any case.

6 strips bacon, coarsely chopped

3 pounds bone-in, skin-on chicken breasts or thighs, or a combination

salt and freshly ground black pepper

6 cubes frozen crushed garlic

½ (16-ounce) bag frozen pearl onions, thawed

½ pound white mushrooms, sliced

2 cups white wine (I like white burgundy)

2 cups chicken broth

several thyme sprigs

chopped fresh parsley, for garnish

GLUTEN-FREE

In a large sauté pan or skillet over medium heat, cook the bacon until the fat is rendered and the bacon is cooked but not quite crisp, about 4 minutes. Remove the bacon with a slotted spoon and drain on a paper towel. Season the chicken with salt and pepper, and working in batches, brown the chicken pieces on both sides, transferring to a plate as you go. Pour off all but 2 tablespoons of fat from the pan. Add the garlic and sauté until fragrant, 2 to 3 minutes. Add the onions and sauté until softened, 3 to 4 minutes. Add the mushrooms and sauté until softened, about 5 minutes. Add the wine and bring to a boil. Lower the heat to medium and simmer until the brown bits are released from the bottom of the pan and the wine is slightly reduced, about 5 minutes. Add the chicken broth, thyme, and bacon. Return the chicken to the pan, cover, and simmer until the chicken is no longer pink, about 30 minutes, turning the chicken once about halfway through. Remove the chicken and vegetables to a platter. Simmer the sauce, uncovered, until reduced by half, 6 to 7 minutes. Season to taste with salt and pepper, and pour over the chicken. Garnish with parsley before serving.

Serves: 4
Prep Time: 10 minutes
Cooking Time: 1 hour

PROVENÇAL CHICKEN

*Provençal ingredients are sunny and bold. Olives, fennel, rosemary—
all bright, fragrant, and full of flavor. The cooking aromas put me in a
great mood way before the food hits the table. The flavors of this sauce
also pair well with fish fillets, especially swordfish or halibut.*

1 tablespoon salt

1 teaspoon freshly ground black pepper

½ teaspoon dried thyme

3 to 4 pounds bone-in, skin-on chicken breasts or thighs, or a combination

1 tablespoon olive oil

1 medium onion, thinly sliced

1 bulb fennel, thinly sliced

4 cubes frozen crushed garlic

1 cup white wine

2 sprigs fresh rosemary

½ cup chicken broth

1 (15-ounce) can chopped tomatoes in juice

1 cup black or green olives, or a combination

Preheat the oven to 400°F. In a small bowl, combine the salt, pepper, and thyme. Use this spice mixture to season the chicken. In a large sauté pan or skillet, heat the olive oil over high heat. Working in batches, brown the chicken on both sides, transferring to an ovenproof baking dish as you go. Pour off all but 2 tablespoons of fat from the pan, and sauté the onion and fennel until tender, 3 to 4 minutes. Add the garlic and sauté until fragrant, 1 to 2 minutes. Add the wine and bring to a boil, then lower the heat to medium and simmer until the brown bits are released from the bottom of the pan and the wine reduces slightly, 5 minutes. While the sauce is simmering, remove the leaves from one rosemary sprig, finely chop, and set aside. Add the chicken broth and tomatoes, along with the remaining rosemary sprig, to the sauce. Pour the sauce over the chicken, and roast in the oven until the chicken is no longer pink in the center, 25 to 35 minutes. Add the olives in the last 5 minutes of cooking to warm them. Adjust the seasoning with salt and pepper. Remove the rosemary sprig from the sauce. Scatter the chopped rosemary over the chicken before serving.

Serves: 4 to 6
Prep Time: 10 minutes
Cooking Time: 1 hour

For fish, skip the browning step, and either simmer or roast the fillets in the sauce until cooked through. Depending on the thickness of the fish, 10 to 12 minutes should do it.

VIGNERON'S SAUSAGES

This dish has a great rustic look to it, and flavor for days. It's the type of simple recipe you'll make many times. Just toss a salad, pour the wine, and bon appétit! *I like the TJ's Italian Sweet Sausages or Italian Hot Sausages for this dish—not very French, but very tasty.*

1 pound fresh (not cured) beef, pork, or chicken sausages

1 tablespoon butter

2 shallots, thinly sliced

1 cup white burgundy (or other dry chardonnay)

2 tablespoons Dijon mustard

1 cup seedless green or red grapes, or a combination

salt and freshly ground black pepper

Preheat the oven to 400°F. In a medium sauté pan or skillet over medium-high heat, cover the sausages with water and simmer 10 minutes. While the sausages poach, dot the butter over the bottom of a 9 x 9-inch ovenproof casserole dish. Sprinkle the shallots over the butter, and when the sausages have cooked for 10 minutes (they will not be completely cooked through), place them on top of the shallots. Pour the wine over the sausages and bake until no longer pink in the center, about 35 minutes, turning halfway through the cooking time so that the sausages brown evenly. Remove the sausages and keep warm. Pour the wine-shallot mixture into the sauté pan or skillet, bring to a boil over medium-high heat, and stir in the mustard. Simmer until thickened, about 4 minutes, then add the grapes and simmer until just warmed through. Season to taste with salt and pepper, pour the sauce over the sausages, and serve.

Serves: 4
Prep Time: 5 minutes
Cooking Time: 45 minutes

BURGUNDY POACHED PEARS

Simple, elegant, easy, and chocolaty. Meets my criteria for the perfect dessert. Plus, there's fruit, so it's health food, right? The poaching liquid is reusable, and it gets better with each use. Keep it frozen between poachings (in a plastic container or sealable plastic bag) and reuse. The liquid will pick up flavor from the fruit each time. You may need to add a bit more wine and sugar if you have removed some of the syrup to reduce for sauce, as in this recipe.

1 (750-ml) bottle burgundy

1½ cups sugar

several grinds black pepper

4 pears, peeled

1 (10-ounce) jar Trader Joe's Hot Fudge Sauce, warmed in a microwave or pan of simmering water

VEGETARIAN

In a large saucepan over high heat, bring the wine, sugar, and pepper to a boil. Lower the heat and simmer until the sugar is dissolved, about 5 minutes. Place the pears in the poaching liquid and cook until tender, about 20 minutes. The cooking time will depend on the ripeness and size of the pears. The fruit is ready when it yields easily to a skewer and when it has colored slightly from the wine. Transfer the pears from the poaching liquid to dessert plates.

In a small saucepan, bring 1 cup of the poaching liquid to a vigorous boil over high heat, and reduce to a syrupy consistency. Pour the syrup over the pears, and generously drizzle the hot fudge sauce on top.

Serves: 4
Prep Time: 5 minutes
Cooking Time: 30 minutes

....

Note that this recipe calls for pear halves, but sliced pears may also be used and will take 5 to 10 minutes to cook. Other fruits, such as peaches, may be substituted for the pears.

....

Use a cheap, but drinkable, bottle of burgundy.

....

LIGHTNING QUICK ALMOND CAKE

This is a quick and easy cake that is great for dessert or for snacking. Even better with a pot of tea and a couple best friends. In place of the raspberry preserves, you can use apricot, or just about any fruit you like. If you don't want to gild the lily, skip the raspberry and chocolate garnishes, and dust the cake with powdered sugar.

½ cup Trader Joe's Just Almond Meal

1 cup flour

2 teaspoons baking powder

pinch of salt

1 cup sugar

½ cup plain yogurt

3 eggs

½ teaspoon vanilla or almond extract

½ cup canola oil

½ cup Trader Joe's Fresh Raspberry Preserves

¾ cup Trader Joe's Hot Fudge Sauce

VEGETARIAN

Preheat the oven to 350°F and butter a 9-inch cake pan. In a medium bowl, combine the almond meal, flour, baking powder, and salt. Place the sugar in a large bowl and stir in the yogurt, eggs, and vanilla or almond extract with a spatula or wooden spoon until combined. Stir in the dry ingredients, then add the canola oil. Stir until incorporated, then pour the batter into the prepared pan. Bake until golden and slightly pulling away from the sides of the pan, about 25 minutes. Cool 10 minutes in the pan before unmolding. Melt the preserves in a saucepan (or the microwave) until spreadable, and spread on top of the cake. Spread the hot fudge sauce onto the sides of the cake.

Serves: 8 to 10

Prep Time: 10 minutes

Cooking Time: 25 minutes

BELLA ITALIA

- POTATO-KALE MINESTRA
- MEATBALL MINESTRA
- SICILIAN LEMON SALAD
- CRACKED POTATOES WITH ROSEMARY
- PANZANELLA
- TORTA DI PORRI (LEEK TART)
- PASTA MOLLICA
- RED WINE PASTA
- LEFTOVER PASTA FRITTATA
- PENNE DI PISTACHE
- CHICKEN CAPONATA
- TAGLIATA CON RUCOLA
- SWORDFISH SICILIANA
- AFFOGATO

As in most Mediterranean climates, Italian cuisine relies primarily on fresh, seasonal ingredients, simply prepared. Works for me, especially on busy evenings. At my house, a quick pasta dish—some sautéed fresh vegetables with a glug of great olive oil and a dusting of Tuscan pepper cheese—will always beat take-out, and the meal goes together as fast as ordering at a drive-through window. TJ's carries the only prepared polenta I love, as well as some interesting dried pastas and jarred sauces. *Vino italiano*? *Si, certamente*!

POTATO-KALE MINESTRA

You won't be sorry if you simmer up a pot of this at the first sign of rain. It's one of those comfort-in-a-bowl dishes that makes you feel good about snuggling inside all day.

1 tablespoon olive oil

½ pound Trader Joe's Smoked Andouille Chicken Sausage, sliced ½ inch thick

1 medium onion, chopped

2 cubes frozen crushed garlic

1 tablespoon minced fresh rosemary leaves, minced

1 pound russet potatoes, cubed

rind of Parmesan cheese (optional)

4 cups chicken or vegetable broth

2 cups Trader Joe's Kale, Southern Greens Blend, or Chard of Many Colors, chopped

salt and freshly ground black pepper

grated Parmesan cheese, for garnish

GLUTEN-FREE

Heat the olive oil in a medium saucepan over medium-high heat. Sauté the sausages until browned, about 4 minutes. Set the sausages aside. In the same pan, sauté the onion until fragrant and softened, 5 to 6 minutes. Add the garlic and sauté until fragrant, about 2 minutes. Add the rosemary, potatoes, and cheese rind, if using, and broth. Bring the liquid to a boil, lower the heat, and simmer about 10 minutes. Add the sausage and simmer until the potatoes are tender, about 10 minutes. Add the greens and simmer until wilted and tender, about 5 minutes longer. Season to taste with salt and pepper. Remove the rind, if used. Ladle into bowls and pass the Parmesan cheese.

Serves: 4 to 6
Prep Time: 10 minutes
Cooking Time: less than an hour

MEATBALL MINESTRA

Couldn't be faster, or more flavorful! Those TJ's meatballs carry tons of flavor, which permeates the broth as they simmer. Love it for lunch, or as a first course for an Italian meal.

3 cups chicken broth

1 (12-ounce) package Trader Joe's Gourmet Chicken Meatballs with Sun-Dried Tomatoes, Basil, and Provolone

handful of arugula

salt and freshly ground black pepper

Toscano Cheese with Black Pepper, for garnish

GLUTEN-FREE

In a medium saucepan, bring the chicken broth to a boil over high heat. Add the meatballs and simmer until warmed through, about 5 minutes. Add the arugula and cook until wilted, 2 to 3 minutes. Season to taste with salt and pepper. Ladle into bowls and grate some cheese over each portion.

Serves: 4
Prep Time: 5 minutes
Cooking Time: 10 minutes

SICILIAN LEMON SALAD

I just love the bright simplicity of this salad. Meyer lemons make their appearance in late winter, and their sweet-tartness is perfect for spotlighting in this dish.

2 Meyer lemons

1 (4-ounce) bag mâche lettuce, or ½ (7-ounce) bag arugula

½ medium red onion, thinly sliced

2 green onions, thinly sliced

salt and freshly ground black pepper

¼ cup olive oil

VEGAN, GLUTEN-FREE

Cut both ends off the lemons. Set a lemon on one end on a cutting board, and using a sharp paring knife, follow the curve of the lemon from top to bottom, cutting off the peel and pith. Repeat with the other lemon. Over a bowl to catch the juice, cut between the membranes, removing the segments of flesh from both lemons. Discard the membranes and reserve the extra juice. Toss the greens with the red onion, green onions, and lemon segments. Lightly salt the salad, then add any reserved lemon juice and the olive oil and toss again. Adjust the seasoning with salt and pepper.

Serves: 4
Prep Time: 10 minutes
Cooking Time: none

CRACKED POTATOES *with* ROSEMARY

These are so much fun. I let my guests do the "smushing"—boil up the spuds, give your friends a glass of wine, and let them take over. But smush gently: You don't want hand-smashed potatoes, just gently flattened ones. These are great hot or at room temperature. They make sought-after leftovers—my favorite breakfast involves a sauté pan and these potatoes with an egg scrambled in.

1 pound new potatoes, unpeeled

¼ cup olive oil

1 tablespoon chopped fresh rosemary

salt and freshly ground black pepper

VEGAN

In a medium saucepan, steam or boil the potatoes until barely tender, 12 to 15 minutes (depending on size). When the potatoes are cool enough to handle, place them on a flat surface, and gently press down with your hand on each potato to compress it. The skin will crack as the potato flattens and spreads. Heat the olive oil in a large sauté pan or skillet over medium heat. Add the rosemary and a single layer of potatoes (work in batches if your pan is not large enough to accommodate all the potatoes in a single layer), and cook without stirring, until the bottoms of the potatoes are golden, about 5 minutes. With tongs or a spoon, turn the potatoes over, and cook until the other side is golden and the potatoes are tender, 3 to 4 minutes longer. Transfer to a serving platter and repeat with the remaining potatoes, if necessary. Season to taste with salt and pepper.

Serves: 4
Prep Time: 10 minutes
Cooking Time: 25 minutes

PANZANELLA

I've heard that panzanella *means "little swamp" in Italian. Whatever the direct translation, it means summer to me. Don't even think of making this unless the tomatoes are gorgeous—pink, hard tomatoes just won't cut it here!*

2 medium ripe tomatoes, cubed

1 Persian cucumber, thinly sliced

½ medium red onion, thinly sliced

½ cup extra-virgin olive oil

2 tablespoons red wine vinegar

¼ cup fresh basil leaves, torn

fresh mint leaves (optional)

¾ (1-pound) loaf day-old artisanal bread, cut into 1-inch cubes

salt and freshly ground black pepper

VEGAN

Combine the tomatoes, cucumber, and onion in a large bowl. Add the olive oil, vinegar, basil, and mint, if using, and toss. Add the bread cubes, toss again to combine the ingredients, and season to taste with salt and pepper.

Serves: 4
Prep Time: 10 minutes
Cooking Time: none

. . . .

A one-pound loaf of Trader Joe's Pain Pascal Organic Demi Miche, Pain Rustique, or another hearty bread, trimmed of crust, will work well in this recipe.

. . . .

TORTA DI PORRI (LEEK TART)

A great first course, or a rich and decadent side. I also love a slice served over lightly dressed greens as a simple but satisfying dinner. TJ's pie crust (found in the frozen-food section) comes two to a package, but you'll need only one for this recipe; keep the other reserved in the freezer for another use.

1 Trader Joe's Gourmet Pie Crust, thawed

2 tablespoons butter

1 (16-ounce) bag frozen sliced leeks, thawed

¼ cup pinot grigio or another dry white wine

4 eggs

½ cup cream

½ teaspoon dried thyme

salt and freshly ground black pepper

1½ cups Trader Joe's Swiss and Gruyère Shredded Cheese Blend, divided

VEGETARIAN

Preheat the oven to 375°F. On a floured surface, roll the pie dough out to mend any cracks, and press it into a 9-inch removable-bottom tart pan. Place a sheet of foil or parchment over the dough, and cover with pie weights or dried beans. Bake 15 minutes. Carefully remove the weights and foil or parchment and return the pan to the oven. Bake until the crust is golden, 8 to 10 minutes longer. Cool to room temperature.

In a medium sauté pan or skillet over high heat, melt the butter. Sauté the leeks until tender and the slices begin to separate, about 5 minutes. Add the wine and boil until the pan is nearly dry, 3 to 4 minutes. Transfer to a large bowl and cool to room temperature. Crack the eggs into a small bowl and whisk in the cream. Add the thyme and season lightly with salt and pepper. Combine the egg mixture with the cooled leeks, stirring to combine. Scatter ½ cup cheese over the surface of the tart crust, and stir the remaining 1 cup cheese into the leek mixture. Fill the tart shell with the leek mixture, and bake until set, about 25 minutes. Cool slightly before slicing.

Serves: 6 to 8
Prep Time: 10 minutes
Cooking Time: 1 hour

GREEK FLAVORS CHICKEN

This dish packs a punch of Mediterranean flavor. The sharp, salty feta and the briny green olives or supple marinated sun-dried tomatoes will have you dreaming of evenings in Athens—real or imagined. In a dinner emergency, boneless chicken breasts will work, too. But their flavor pales in comparison to the bone-in version.

4 bone-in, skin-on chicken breasts

salt and freshly ground black pepper

1 tablespoon olive oil

4 ounces crumbled feta cheese

½ (10-ounce) jar Trader Joe's Green Olive Tapenade, or ½ (8 ½-ounce jar) Trader Joe's Julienne Sliced Sun-Dried Tomatoes

1 cup dry white wine

1 cup chicken broth

GLUTEN-FREE

Lightly season the chicken with salt and pepper. In a medium sauté pan or skillet, heat the olive oil over high heat. Cook the breasts skin side down until browned, 4 to 5 minutes. Turn the breasts over and brown on the other side, 3 to 4 minutes more. Remove the pan from the heat and transfer the chicken to a cutting board to cool slightly. In a small bowl, combine the feta and tapenade or sun-dried tomatoes. Using a paring knife, cut a deep pocket about 4 inches long in each chicken breast and stuff some of the feta mixture inside each one. Mound any additional filling atop the chicken. Return the sauté pan or skillet to the stovetop and add the white wine. Bring to a boil, lower the heat to medium, and simmer 5 minutes. Add the chicken broth and the chicken, skin-side up. Simmer, covered, until the liquid is reduced to a saucy consistency and the chicken is no longer pink in the center, about 25 minutes.

Serves: 4
Prep Time: 5 minutes
Cooking Time: 45 minutes

MEDITERRANEAN MEATBALLS

These little flavor bombs are great in sandwiches, over orzo or other pasta, or on skewers for party fare.

1 cup fresh bread crumbs

½ cup chicken broth

1½ pounds ground dark meat, or a combination of white and dark meat, turkey

½ (7-ounce) container refrigerated Trader Joe's Traditional Olive Tapenade

½ (6-ounce) container Trader Joe's Crumbled Feta with Mediterranean Herbs

freshly ground black pepper

In a large bowl, combine the bread crumbs and chicken broth. Let stand for 10 minutes to allow the crumbs to absorb the liquid. Add the ground turkey, tapenade, and feta and combine well. Season with black pepper. Refrigerate the turkey mixture for 20 minutes. Preheat the oven to 400°F. Form the turkey meatballs about the size of walnuts; you should have about 24. Place on a rimmed baking sheet. Bake until the meatballs are no longer pink in the center, about 25 minutes.

Serves: 4 to 6
Prep Time: 15 minutes
Cooking Time: 35 minutes

YOGURT-SLATHERED GRILLED LAMB

Build a summer evening around this easy entrée. Sip cocktails while the lamb marinates and grills, then set up a table outside for assembling plates of deliciousness. The livin' will certainly be easy.

1 (.75-ounce) package fresh mint

1 cup plain yogurt

4 cubes frozen crushed garlic

1 boneless leg of lamb, netting removed (about 4 pounds)

salt and freshly ground black pepper

1 medium red onion, thinly sliced

2 Persian cucumbers, sliced

2 medium tomatoes, sliced

whole wheat pita bread

GLUTEN-FREE (IF SERVED WITHOUT PITA BREAD)

Remove the stems from the mint and chop the leaves. Set half aside. In a small bowl, mix the remaining mint leaves with the yogurt and garlic. Lay the lamb flat on a work surface and season the lamb with salt and pepper. Slather the yogurt mixture all over the surface of the meat. Let marinate for 30 minutes. Heat a grill to medium. Grill the lamb until medium-rare, about 10 minutes per side. Let stand 10 minutes before slicing thinly. Serve with onion, cucumbers, tomatoes, pita bread, and the reserved mint.

Serves: 8

Prep Time: 5 minutes, plus marinating time

Cooking Time: 30 minutes

FRUIT BATHED *in* WATERMELON

Just about the most refreshing way I can think of to end a summer meal.

5 cups seeded watermelon cubes

¼ cup Moscato or another sweet white dessert wine, or sparkling wine

1 to 2 tablespoons honey

1 pound ripe peaches or nectarines, peeled and sliced

1 cup fresh blackberries, raspberries, or strawberries, or a combination

mint sprigs, for garnish

VEGETARIAN, GLUTEN-FREE

In a food processor or blender, puree the watermelon cubes with the wine and honey. Refrigerate. Arrange the sliced peaches and the berries in shallow bowls, and pour some of the watermelon sauce over each. Garnish with mint leaves.

Serves: 6

Prep Time: 10 minutes

Cooking Time: none

Adding a swirl of plain or vanilla yogurt or a scoop of frozen yogurt would be delish!

EASTERN EUROPEAN

- BEETS WITH ORANGE
- HOT POTATO SALAD WITH BACON DRESSING
- WARM MUSHROOM SALAD
- GREEN BEANS WITH PEARS AND BACON
- BAVARIAN-STYLE MUSHROOMS
- STUFFED BELL PEPPERS
- MAMALIGA (ROMANIAN POLENTA WITH FETA)
- FRAT BRATS
- CHICKEN WITH APRICOTS
- APRICOT LINZER BARS
- CHILLED PEACH SOUP

These recipes are seasoned travelers—you might find versions of them in Munich, Prague, or Budapest. You'll find hearty dishes to get you through a cold winter. The food I've enjoyed in this part of the world relies on simple seasonal ingredients that are treated with respect and not too fussed over. My kind of food, and I hope yours, too!

BEETS WITH ORANGE

Couldn't be easier, and looks so pretty. I love the convenience of the TJ's precooked beets. Since I'm the only beet lover in my house, this treat is all mine.

2 (8-ounce) packages Trader Joe's Steamed and Peeled Baby Beets

grated zest and juice of 1 medium orange

2 tablespoons Trader Joe's Orange Muscat Champagne Vinegar or red wine vinegar

¼ cup olive oil

salt and freshly ground black pepper

dollop of crème fraîche (optional)

VEGETARIAN, VEGAN (IF SERVED WITHOUT CRÈME FRAÎCHE), GLUTEN-FREE

Toss the beets with the orange zest and juice, vinegar, and olive oil. Season to taste with salt and pepper. Serve with a dollop of crème fraîche, if using.

Serves: 4 to 6
Prep Time: 5 minutes
Cooking Time: none

HOT POTATO SALAD *with* BACON DRESSING

I'm not sure how strictly authentic this recipe is, but I am certain it's delicious!

1½ pounds red potatoes, unpeeled

salt and freshly ground black pepper

6 strips bacon

6 green onions, sliced

½ cup red wine vinegar

2 teaspoons sugar

GLUTEN-FREE

Place the potatoes in a medium saucepan and cover with cold water. Salt the water and bring to a boil over high heat. Cook the potatoes until a fork pierces them easily, 10 to 12 minutes. Meanwhile, in a sauté pan over medium-high heat, cook the bacon until crisp. Transfer the bacon to paper towels and set aside. Pour the bacon fat into a heatproof measuring cup and discard all but ¼ cup. Drain the potatoes and cool just enough to handle. Slice the potatoes ¼ inch thick and toss with the green onions. Return the reserved bacon fat to the sauté pan. Add the vinegar and sugar, and bring to a boil over high heat. Reduce the heat to medium and simmer until the strong vinegar aroma softens and the dressing thickens slightly, about 2 minutes. Pour over the potatoes. Crumble in the bacon and season to taste with salt and pepper.

Serves: 4 to 6
Prep Time: 5 minutes
Cooking Time: 30 minutes

WARM MUSHROOM SALAD

Mushroom hunting is a family affair in many areas of the world, and the prime spots are closely guarded secrets. In many areas of Europe, the local pharmacy is a great resource for identifying edible mushrooms. While I don't recommend harvesting wild mushrooms—unless you absolutely know what you're doing—I can enthusiastically recommend making this recipe with any mushroom TJ's carries.

2 ounces bacon or pancetta, chopped

1 medium shallot, thinly sliced

8 ounces fresh mushrooms, sliced (I like a mix of crimini, shiitake, and portobellas)

salt and freshly ground black pepper

2 tablespoons red wine vinegar

½ (7.5-ounce) container crème fraîche

1 (5-ounce) bag mixed baby greens, such as Trader Joe's Baby Spring Mix or Herb Salad Mix

handful of shredded carrots

GLUTEN-FREE

Sauté the bacon or pancetta over medium-high heat in a medium sauté pan or skillet until beginning to crisp, about 3 minutes. Add the shallot and sauté until fragrant, about 1 minute longer. Add the mushrooms and lower the heat to medium. Continue to sauté for 5 to 6 minutes. (At first, the mushrooms will absorb the bacon drippings and will appear dry. After a few minutes, they will release some of their juices and will appear moister. At this point, they will begin to soften and cook.) Season the mushrooms with salt and pepper as they cook. When the mushrooms are tender, add the vinegar and cook for 2 minutes. Add the crème fraîche and warm through. Adjust the seasoning with salt and pepper. Arrange the greens on a platter and scatter the shredded carrots over them. Top with the warm mushrooms. They'll wilt the greens slightly, and the sauce will dress the salad.

Serves: 4
Prep Time: 15 minutes
Cooking Time: less than 15 minutes

A slice of bacon is about 1 ounce, so two will do nicely for this recipe. You might want to cook an extra slice for the cook's treat!

GREEN BEANS *with* PEARS *and* BACON

Something about this combination just makes me smile. The sweetness of the pears, the salty smoke of the bacon, and the good-for-you greenness of the beans all come together in a great way. I'll eat this as a side, as a salad for lunch, cold or hot, or I'll toss leftovers into a frittata. Great with a handful of walnuts or pecans tossed in at the end.

1 cup chicken broth

1 pound green beans, trimmed

4 strips bacon

1 tablespoon butter

1 medium red onion, thinly sliced

1 medium pear, chopped

salt and freshly ground black pepper

GLUTEN-FREE

In a medium sauté pan or skillet over high heat, bring the chicken broth to a boil. Add the green beans and simmer until nearly tender, about 6 minutes. When the broth is nearly gone and the beans are softened, remove them from the pan. In the same pan, cook the bacon until crisp. Transfer to paper towels and set aside. Pour off all but 1 tablespoon of the bacon fat and discard. Add the butter and sauté the onion until just tender, about 4 minutes. Add the pear and sauté until softened and fragrant, 3 to 4 minutes. Add the green beans back to the pan, tossing to combine. Season to taste with salt and pepper, and crumble the bacon over the top.

Serves: 4
Prep Time: 10 minutes
Cooking Time: 20 minutes

You could also use pancetta or chopped ham in place of the bacon.

BAVARIAN-STYLE MUSHROOMS

These winter-wonderful mushroom morsels are great as a vegetable dish, tossed with pasta, or served with brats or the tasty little Nuremburg sausages Trader Joe's has carried recently.

2 tablespoons butter

1 medium shallot, chopped

1 (12-ounce) bag sliced crimini mushrooms

½ cup beef or chicken broth

½ cup dry white wine

½ cup crème fraîche

salt and freshly ground black pepper

chopped fresh parsley, for garnish

VEGETARIAN, GLUTEN-FREE

In a medium sauté pan or skillet, heat the butter to sizzling over medium-high heat. Sauté the shallot until fragrant, 2 to 3 minutes. Add the mushrooms and sauté about 8 minutes. (At first the mushrooms will soak up all the butter, and the pan will look nearly dry. Keep cooking until the mushrooms release their liquid and the liquid evaporates.) Add the broth and wine, and bring to a boil over high heat. Lower the heat to medium and simmer until slightly reduced, 2 to 3 minutes. Stir in the crème fraîche and warm through. Season to taste with salt and pepper, and garnish with parsley.

Serves: 4
Prep Time: 5 minutes
Cooking Time: 15 minutes

STUFFED BELL PEPPERS

Let's call this a template recipe. There are so many variations on this theme—you probably grew up with one. Add sautéed ground beef or turkey to the stuffing, and maybe some tomato sauce. Use brown or white rice instead of the quinoa, switch up the cheese you use to top the peppers, or leave it off. You get the idea: Hollow out some peppers, put some good stuff inside, and bake 'em up. Easy, yummy stuff.

3 medium bell peppers

salt and freshly ground black pepper

1 (16-ounce) bag frozen Trader Joe's Quinoa Duo

1 cup chicken broth, vegetable broth, or water

1 cup shredded cheese, like Trader Joe's Shredded Smoked Cheese Blend

VEGETARIAN (IF VEGETABLE BROTH OR WATER IS USED), GLUTEN-FREE

Preheat the oven to 350°F. Cut the bell peppers in half from stem to bottom, and scrape out the seeds and membranes. Place the pepper halves in an ovenproof baking dish large enough to hold them in a single layer. Season the interior of the peppers with salt and pepper. Divide the quinoa mixture evenly among the peppers. Drizzle a little of the broth or water over each pepper, and pour the rest into the bottom of the pan. Scatter the cheese over the quinoa. Cover the pan with foil and bake until the peppers are tender, about 40 minutes. Remove the foil and bake until the peppers are soft and the cheese is melted, about 10 minutes longer.

Serves: 6
Prep Time: 5 minutes
Cooking Time: less than 1 hour

MAMALIGA (ROMANIAN POLENTA *with* FETA)

The world over, polenta seems to show up on peasant tables. Inexpensive, filling, and compatible with lots of different flavors, polenta is a pantry must-have. The TJ's premade polenta rolls make prep ridiculously quick. This dish is also traditionally served with sautéed sausage in the middle or on top of the polenta rounds. Hot or mild Italian sausage would be tasty.

1 (16-ounce) roll Trader Joe's Organic Polenta

¾ cup crumbled feta cheese

½ cup crème fraîche

freshly ground black pepper

VEGETARIAN, GLUTEN-FREE

Preheat the oven to 375°F. Cut the polenta into ½-inch rounds. Layer half the polenta in the bottom of an ovenproof shallow casserole. Crumble the feta evenly over the surface of each polenta round and top with most of the crème fraîche, reserving about 2 tablespoons. Season with pepper. Cover the cheese with the remaining polenta and spread the reserved crème fraîche on top. Season with additional pepper. Bake until warmed through, about 30 minutes. Cool 10 minutes before serving.

Serves: 4
Prep Time: 5 minutes
Cooking Time: 30 minutes

FRAT BRATS

Bratwurst and beer—is there more that needs to be said? You can use whatever beer you like. Simmering the sausages in beer adds great flavor, and tossing onions into the brew creates meltingly tender toppings for the sandwiches.

1 (16-ounce) package Trader Joe's Hofbrau Brats (bratwurst)

2 medium red onions, thinly sliced

1 (12-ounce) beer

4 focaccia or panini rolls

about ½ cup Trader Joe's Corn and Chile Tomato-Less Salsa

GARNISHES:

sliced avocado

sliced Muenster or Havarti cheese

sliced tomatoes

Place the bratwurst and onions in a medium sauté pan or skillet and pour the beer over them. Bring the beer to a boil over high heat and simmer the bratwurst for 5 minutes. Turn the sausages over and continue to cook until the beer is nearly evaporated and the onions begin to soften and deepen in color, about 10 minutes. Remove the onions and set aside. Cook the bratwurst until lightly browned on one side, then turn to brown lightly on the other side. Remove from the pan and cool slightly. Cut the sausages in half lengthwise. (If they are not cooked enough for your liking, return them to the pan, cut side down, for a few minutes to cook them more thoroughly.) Split the rolls (like hamburger buns) and arrange a bratwurst on the bottom of each roll. Place some of the onions on top of each, and add a dollop of corn salsa. Garnish as desired with avocado, cheese, and tomatoes.

Serves: 4
Prep Time: 5 minutes
Cooking Time: less than 20 minutes

CHICKEN *with* APRICOTS

What a simple dish, but packed with loads of flavor. The dried apricots carry such a concentrated pop of sweet-sour sunshine, this dish will bring a few rays to a dreary evening's dinner.

½ (16-ounce) bag dried apricots, chopped

1½ cups hot chicken broth

3 pounds bone-in, skin-on chicken breasts or thighs, or a combination

salt and freshly ground black pepper

2 tablespoons olive oil

1 medium onion, chopped

½ teaspoon ground cinnamon

½ cup dry white wine

juice of 1 lemon

GLUTEN-FREE

Preheat the oven to 400°F. In a heatproof bowl, cover the apricots with the hot chicken broth (add some water if needed to submerge the fruit). Let stand 15 minutes. Season the chicken with salt and pepper. In a large sauté pan or skillet, heat the olive oil over high heat. Brown the chicken on all sides. Transfer the chicken to a rimmed baking sheet and roast in the oven until no longer pink in the center, about 30 minutes. While the chicken roasts, pour off all but 1 tablespoon of drippings from the sauté pan or skillet and sauté the onion until softened, 3 to 4 minutes. Drain the apricots, reserving the liquid, and add the apricots to the pan. Add the cinnamon and wine, and bring to a boil. Boil for 2 minutes. Add the reserved apricot soaking liquid and simmer until thickened, about 5 minutes. Season the sauce to taste with lemon juice, salt, and pepper, and serve over the chicken.

Serves: 4

Prep Time: 5 minutes, plus soaking time for apricots

Cooking Time: under 1 hour

APRICOT LINZER BARS

A little square of this buttery, jammy treat and a cup of tea make an afternoon just about perfect. These little squares are also delicious with raspberry preserves instead of apricot. Powdered sugar is seasonal at TJ's. Stock up when you find it.

12 tablespoons butter, at room temperature, plus more for coating the dish

½ cup brown sugar

1 egg

¼ teaspoon ground cinnamon

pinch of ground nutmeg

pinch of salt

2 cups all-purpose flour

1 cup Trader Joe's Just Almond Meal

1 cup Trader Joe's Fresh Apricot Preserves

grated zest and juice of 1 lemon

½ teaspoon vanilla extract

powdered sugar, for garnish (optional)

VEGETARIAN

Preheat the oven to 350°F. Butter an 8 x 8-inch baking dish. With an electric mixer, beat the butter and brown sugar until fluffy, about 5 minutes. Beat in the egg, cinnamon, nutmeg, and salt. In a medium bowl, stir together the flour and almond meal, then add to the butter mixture. Stir just to combine well. Press three-quarters of the dough into the bottom of the prepared pan and about 1 inch up the sides. In a small bowl, stir together the preserves, lemon zest and juice, and vanilla, and spread over the surface of the dough. Roll the remaining dough into thin ropes or "snakes"—like Play-Doh—and arrange in a lattice pattern over the preserves. Bake until the filling is set and the crust is golden, about 40 minutes. Cool to room temperature and dust with powdered sugar, if using.

Serves: 6 to 8
Prep Time: 10 minutes
Cooking Time: 40 minutes

CHILLED PEACH SOUP

In summer, TJ's gets great, drip-down-your-arm-juicy peaches. That's the time to make this soup. The color will make you fall in love, and the flavor is summer in a bowl.

2 cups brown sugar

2 cups water

6 gloriously ripe, fragrant peaches

grated zest and juice of 1 lemon

3 tablespoons granulated sugar

2 cups sweet white wine like moscato, or a sweet riesling or gewurztraminer

¼ teaspoon ground cinnamon

pinch of ground nutmeg

pinch of salt

¼ cup plum brandy

1 cup heavy whipping cream

VEGETARIAN, GLUTEN-FREE

In a medium saucepan, stir the brown sugar into the water. Bring to a boil over high heat, lower the heat to medium, and simmer until the sugar is dissolved, about 8 minutes. Set aside to cool. Peel and coarsely chop the peaches. Toss half the peaches with half the lemon juice and the granulated sugar. Set aside. In a food processor or blender, combine the remaining peaches with the lemon zest and remaining lemon juice and the cooled brown sugar syrup. Purée. Add the wine, cinnamon, nutmeg, salt, and brandy, and pulse to combine. Refrigerate until cold. Before serving, chill a medium bowl and a whisk or the beaters of an electric mixer. Whip the cream until stiff peaks form. Fold the whipped cream into the peach puree and garnish with the remaining chopped peaches.

Serves: 6 to 8
Prep Time: 10 minutes
Cooking Time: 10 minutes

AFRICAN ADVENTURE

- **PEANUT SOUP**
- **MOROCCAN SWEET POTATO AND SQUASH STEW**
- **SPICY COCONUT RICE**
- **JOLLOF RICE**
- **SIZZLING CILANTRO SHRIMP**
- **PALAVER CHICKEN**
- **SENEGALESE CHICKEN**

Africa is on my must-do travel list. The cuisines are as varied as the people inhabiting the vast continent. Many African dishes are quick to make, as cooking fuel is sometimes hard to come by and expensive, and the climate often doesn't allow for long hours in a hot kitchen. That suits me just fine, and I'm guessing wherever you're cooking, a few fast recipes with big flavor will find a place in your kitchen, too.

PEANUT SOUP

Plentiful, inexpensive, and a good source of protein, peanuts play a big role in many of Africa's regional cuisines. This soup is filling and flavorful. It takes only a few minutes of prep and smells great while it simmers, too. The okra goes in at the end of the cooking time— simmering it too long makes it slimy.

1 tablespoon olive oil

1 medium onion, chopped

2 cubes frozen crushed garlic

2 tablespoons minced fresh ginger

2 tablespoons tomato paste

½ teaspoon dried thyme

3 tablespoons creamy peanut butter

6 cups chicken broth, divided

1 cup frozen okra, chopped (optional)

salt and freshly ground black pepper

GLUTEN-FREE

In a medium saucepan, heat the olive oil over medium-high heat. Sauté the onion until fragrant and softened, 3 to 4 minutes. Add the garlic and ginger, and sauté until fragrant, 2 to 3 minutes. Add the tomato paste, stir to combine, and cook 1 to 2 minutes. Add the thyme and peanut butter, and stir to combine. Add about 1 cup chicken broth, and stir until the peanut butter is dissolved. Add the remaining 5 cups broth and bring to a boil. Lower the heat to medium and simmer until slightly reduced, about 30 minutes. Add the okra, if using, and simmer until hot. Season to taste with salt and pepper.

Serves: 6
Prep Time: 5 minutes
Cooking Time: 40 minutes

MOROCCAN SWEET POTATO *and* SQUASH STEW

This gorgeous and aromatic stew makes a great meal for vegetarians (made with veggie broth, of course) or for Meatless Monday. Also great as a side dish, the vibrant flavors will warm up a chilly evening. You could also throw in some cooked chicken, shrimp, or pork to make a hearty one-pot meal for omnivores.

4 tablespoons butter or olive oil

1 medium onion, chopped

2 cubes frozen crushed garlic

2 teaspoons minced fresh ginger

2 teaspoons curry powder

pinch of cayenne pepper

2 cups vegetable or chicken broth

pinch of saffron

1½ pounds pie pumpkin or butternut squash, peeled and cubed

1 pound sweet potatoes, peeled and cubed

1 tablespoon honey

salt and freshly ground black pepper

1 (.75-ounce) package fresh cilantro, chopped

VEGETARIAN (IF VEGETABLE BROTH IS USED), GLUTEN-FREE

In a medium sauté pan or skillet, heat the butter over medium-high heat until foamy. Sauté the onion until softened, 3 to 4 minutes. Add the garlic, ginger, curry powder, and cayenne, and sauté until fragrant, 2 to 3 minutes. Add the broth and saffron and bring to a boil. Lower the heat to medium, and add the squash, sweet potato, and honey. Season lightly with salt and pepper. Cover and simmer, stirring occasionally, until the vegetables are tender, about 20 minutes. Adjust the seasoning with salt, pepper, and additional cayenne. Garnish with chopped cilantro.

Serves: 4 to 6
Prep Time: 10 minutes
Cooking Time: 30 minutes

SPICY COCONUT RICE

This festive-looking (and tasting) rice is served for celebrations in Cameroon. Great with chicken or other roasted meats, it also makes a tasty vegetarian main or side dish. The coconut milk adds a subtle nuttiness to the fragrant rice.

1 tablespoon grapeseed oil

1 onion, chopped

1 red bell pepper, chopped

2 tablespoons tomato paste

1 (14-ounce) can Trader Joe's Light Coconut Milk

¾ cup water

1 teaspoon dried thyme

pinch of ground nutmeg

pinch of ground cinnamon

1 jalapeño chile, seeded and finely chopped

1½ cups basmati or jasmine rice

salt and freshly ground black pepper

½ (10-ounce) bag shredded carrots

VEGAN, GLUTEN-FREE

In a medium saucepan, heat the grapeseed oil over medium-high heat. Sauté the onion until softened, 2 to 3 minutes. Add the bell pepper and sauté until softened, about 3 minutes. Add the tomato paste and stir to coat the vegetables well and warm the tomato paste, 2 to 3 minutes. Add the coconut milk and water and bring to a boil. Add the thyme, nutmeg, cinnamon, jalapeño, and rice and stir to combine. Season to taste with salt and pepper. Cover, reduce the heat to low, and cook for 15 minutes. Turn the heat off, but don't lift the lid for an additional 10 minutes. Add the carrots, fluff the rice, and adjust the seasoning with salt and pepper.

Serves: 4 to 6
Prep Time: 10 minutes
Cooking Time: 40 minutes

JOLLOF RICE

Maybe the original rice bowl, jollof *means "one pot." A staple meal in West Africa, this dish can be prepared vegetarian or using leftover meat from last night's dinner. It's a great "clean out the fridge" strategy, with an exotic flair. If you have leftover chicken or beef (or other meat) you'd like to add to your* jollof, *mound the cooked rice in a bowl and spoon the warmed meat into the center. Green beans are frequently included in this dish, as are carrots, so if you have a few hanging around in the crisper drawer, toss them in. Lentils or garbanzo beans would work, too. You can cook the rice ahead or use Trader Joe's frozen White Rice Fully Cooked.*

4 tablespoons butter or grapeseed oil

1 medium onion, chopped

1 cup chopped green bell pepper

½ teaspoon ground nutmeg

½ teaspoon ground ginger

1 teaspoon ground cumin

1 jalapeño chile, minced

1 (14.5-ounce) can diced tomatoes

1 (6-ounce) can tomato paste

2 cups water

3 cups cooked long-grain rice (1 cup uncooked)

salt and freshly ground black pepper

VEGETARIAN, VEGAN (IF OIL IS USED), GLUTEN-FREE

In a medium sauté pan or skillet, heat the butter or grapeseed oil over medium-high heat. Sauté the onion until softened, 3 to 4 minutes. Add the bell pepper and sauté 3 to 4 minutes. Add the nutmeg, ginger, cumin, and jalapeño, and sauté 2 minutes. Add the tomatoes, tomato paste, and water, and bring to a boil. Lower the heat to medium and simmer until the flavors are combined and the sauce reduces slightly, about 5 minutes. Toss with the cooked rice. Season to taste with salt and pepper.

Serves: 4
Prep Time: 5 minutes
Cooking Time: 20 minutes

SIZZLING CILANTRO SHRIMP

The flavors of cilantro and cumin are part of North Africa's spice palette, bringing a balance of smoky earthiness and bright, vibrant herbaciousness to the plump shrimp. Don't overcook the shrimp—they take only a few minutes to turn pink in the pan.

2 tablespoons olive oil

3 cubes frozen crushed garlic

1 tablespoon minced fresh ginger

1 jalapeño chile, minced

1 teaspoon ground cumin

1 pound uncooked shrimp, peeled and deveined

1 (.75-ounce) package fresh cilantro, chopped

salt and freshly ground black pepper

1 lime, cut into wedges

GLUTEN-FREE

In a large sauté pan or skillet, heat the olive oil over medium-high heat. Sauté the garlic, ginger, jalapeño, and cumin until fragrant, 2 to 3 minutes. Add the shrimp and sauté until just pink and opaque, 4 to 6 minutes. Toss in the cilantro and season lightly with salt and pepper. Serve with lime wedges to squeeze over individual servings.

Serves: 2 as a main dish, 4 as a first course
Prep Time: 5 minutes
Cooking Time: 10 minutes

PALAVER CHICKEN

The name of this lively flavored dish is said to come from the equally lively debate that ensues over the right way to prepare it. There seem to be as many variations to the basic recipe as there are cooks who love to make it and diners who love to eat it.

2 tablespoons butter

2 tablespoons grapeseed oil

3 cubes frozen crushed garlic

1½ pounds boneless, skinless chicken breasts or thighs, or a combination, cut into strips

1 medium onion, chopped

1 (14.5-ounce) can chopped tomatoes

2 tablespoons creamy peanut butter

2 cups chicken broth, divided

1 teaspoon dried thyme

½ pound fresh or frozen spinach

1 jalapeño chile, seeded and finely chopped

salt and freshly ground black pepper

cooked jasmine, basmati, or brown rice, or sautéed spinach

GLUTEN-FREE

In a large sauté pan or skillet, heat the butter and grapeseed oil over medium-high heat. Sauté the garlic until fragrant, about 2 minutes. Add about half the chicken and sauté just until no longer pink, 3 to 4 minutes. With a slotted spoon, transfer the chicken to a platter. Repeat with the remaining chicken. In the now-empty pan, sauté the onion until softened, 3 to 4 minutes. Add the tomatoes and simmer 5 minutes. Add the peanut butter and 1 cup chicken broth, and stir to combine well. Simmer, stirring, for 5 minutes. Add the remaining 1 cup broth and the thyme, spinach, and jalapeño. Add the chicken and any accumulated juices. Season with salt and pepper, and simmer until the chicken is cooked through, about 10 minutes. Adjust the seasoning with salt and pepper. Serve over rice or spinach.

Serves: 4 to 6
Prep Time: 10 minutes
Cooking Time: 30 minutes

SENEGALESE CHICKEN

The tang of lemon and the zing of jalapeño make this a brightly flavored dish for dinner or a picnic. I love it cold the next day, shredded and piled onto flatbread or into a pita pocket. Tuck in some cilantro sprigs and a few slices of tomato—yum!

½ cup fresh lemon juice (2 to 3 lemons)

¼ cup apple cider vinegar

¼ cup grapeseed oil, divided

2 medium onions, thinly sliced

2 to 3 pounds bone-in, skin-on chicken breasts or thighs, or a combination

salt and freshly ground black pepper

2 fresh thyme sprigs

1 jalapeño chile, seeded and minced

2 cups chicken broth, divided

GLUTEN-FREE

In a medium bowl, combine the lemon juice, vinegar, and 2 tablespoons grapeseed oil. Place the onions and chicken in a large sealable plastic bag or a nonreactive bowl, and pour the marinade over the onions and chicken. Refrigerate for 2 hours, turning twice to redistribute the marinade. Remove the chicken from the marinade and reserve the marinade. Season the chicken lightly with salt and pepper. In a large sauté pan or skillet, heat the remaining 2 tablespoons grapeseed oil over high heat. Working in batches, brown the chicken on all sides. Transfer the pieces to a platter as they are browned. When all the chicken is browned, pour off all but 2 tablespoons of the oil. Remove the onions from the marinade and sauté until tender, 3 to 4 minutes. Add the marinade, thyme, and jalapeño to the pan, and bring to a boil. Reduce the heat to medium-low, and simmer for 2 minutes. Add 1 cup chicken broth and the chicken to the pan, cover, and simmer for 20 minutes. Turn the chicken, add the remaining 1 cup chicken broth, and cover again. Simmer until the chicken is no longer pink in the center and the sauce is thickened slightly, about 20 minutes longer.

Serves: 4

Prep Time: 5 minutes, plus marinating time

Cooking Time: 1 hour

MIDDLE EAST MAGIC

- POMEGRANATE AND CUCUMBER SALAD
- RUZ BIL-LOZ WA BIL-TAMAR (RICE WITH ALMONDS AND DATES)
- TAHDIG
- CHERRY RICE PILAF
- COUSCOUS WITH DRIED FRUIT
- WHOLE WHEAT COUSCOUS TABBOULEH-STYLE
- ISRAELI COUSCOUS
- MUJADARA
- FATTOUSH
- IMAM BAYALDI
- MUHAMMARA
- CHICKEN KABOBS
- EGGS POACHED IN TOMATO SAUCE
- YOGURT CURRIED SHRIMP
- DUKKAH CHICKEN
- FESANJAN (CHICKEN WITH POMEGRANATE-WALNUT SAUCE)

Crisp, cooling salads, smoky cumin-scented grilled meats, nubbly couscous—the Middle Eastern table usually includes platters of brightly colored vegetables, good-for-you grains, and more. Thankfully, you don't have to spend all day preparing such a feast. Take advantage of some of TJ's great frozen dishes, simmer sauces, quick-cooking grains, and dips to assemble an impressive array of flavorful, exotic fare in a hurry. Scatter some rose petals, light some candles, and set the mood for a delicious evening.

POMEGRANATE *and* CUCUMBER SALAD

Crisp and hydrating, this salad looks as refreshing as it tastes. Super easy, especially if you buy the pomegranate seeds in the refrigerated section, instead of seeding a pomegranate yourself. The feta is salty, so go easy when adding additional salt.

4 Persian cucumbers, sliced

1 cup pomegranate seeds

6 green onions, sliced

1 (.75-ounce) package fresh cilantro, chopped

1 lime

¼ cup olive oil

¼ cup crumbled feta

salt and freshly ground black pepper

VEGETARIAN, GLUTEN-FREE

Arrange the cucumber slices on a platter. Scatter the pomegranate seeds, green onions, and cilantro over the top. Squeeze the lime over the garnishes and drizzle with olive oil. Scatter the feta over the salad. Season lightly with salt and generously with black pepper.

Serves: 4

Prep Time: 10 minutes

Cooking Time: none

RUZ BIL-LOZ WA BIL-TAMAR (RICE with ALMONDS and DATES)

Simple enough to make on a weeknight, but exotic enough to make it a special evening. Great with chicken or grilled fish or shrimp. You can cook the rice ahead and reheat, or use the frozen fully cooked Trader Joe's White Rice.

2 tablespoons butter

¼ cup blanched, slivered almonds

½ cup dates, pitted and chopped

¼ cup golden raisins

3 cups cooked hot long-grain white rice (1 cup uncooked)

salt and freshly ground black pepper

VEGETARIAN, GLUTEN-FREE

In a medium sauté pan or skillet, heat the butter over medium heat until foamy. Sauté the almonds, dates, and raisins until the almonds are light golden and the fruits soften, about 5 minutes. Toss with the cooked rice. Season to taste with salt and pepper.

Serves: 4
Prep Time: 5 minutes
Cooking Time: 5 minutes

TAHDIG

I dream about tahdig. *The crispy-crunchy-buttery layer of rice at the bottom of the pan is such a treat that it's offered to favored guests. It's an art form—you have to cook it low and slow, or you'll just have burnt rice and a pot to scrape clean. My culinary theory is that pilafs with broken vermicelli were invented to imitate the texture of* tahdig *(also spelled* tadig*). My favorite recipe for* tahdig *advises serving it with boxing gloves, as everyone will be ready to fight for it!*

1½ cups uncooked basmati rice

8 cups water

1 tablespoon salt

3 tablespoons butter

pinch of saffron, dissolved in 2 tablespoons hot water (optional)

VEGETARIAN, GLUTEN-FREE

Put the rice in a large saucepan, cover with the water, and add the salt. Boil for 10 minutes over high heat. Drain the rice into a colander and rinse with hot water. In the saucepan, melt the butter. Return the rice to the pan and reduce the heat to very low. Cover the pan with a clean kitchen towel and then the lid. Pull the ends of the towel up over the top of the lid. Cook, covered, until the rice is cooked and a crisp crust has formed on the bottom of the pan, about 30 minutes. Pour cold water into a bowl large enough to accommodate the saucepan. Spoon out the loose rice in the center of the pan onto a platter, being careful not to disturb the crust at the bottom of the pan. Dip the bottom of the hot pan into the bowl of cold water to loosen the *tahdig.* Spoon the pieces of rice crust on top of the plate of loose rice. If using, drizzle the saffron and water over the rice and *tahdig.* Serve.

Serves: 4
Prep Time: 15 minutes
Cooking Time: 35 minutes

CHERRY RICE PILAF

I love the crunch of the walnuts, the chewiness of the dried cherries, and the earthiness of the thyme in this dish. When I make this with frozen brown rice from TJ's, I feel full of healthful virtue. Cook the rice ahead and reheat, or use Trader Joe's frozen White or Brown Rice Fully Cooked.

2 tablespoons butter

1 medium red onion, chopped

1 cup chopped celery

½ cup dried cherries

½ cup chopped walnuts

1 teaspoon dried thyme

3 cups cooked hot white or brown rice (1 cup uncooked)

salt and freshly ground black pepper

VEGETARIAN, GLUTEN-FREE

In a medium sauté pan or skillet, melt the butter over medium heat. Sauté the onion, celery, cherries, walnuts, and thyme until the onion and celery are tender, about 8 minutes. Add the cooked rice, season to taste with salt and pepper, and toss to combine. Cook until warmed through, about 2 minutes.

Serves: 2 to 4
Prep Time: 5 minutes
Cooking Time: 10 minutes

COUSCOUS *with* DRIED FRUIT

Couscous is amazingly quick to cook and takes so many flavors well. Toss in a handful of toasted nuts, a few chopped dried fruits, or some roasted or sautéed vegetables, and you've got a tasty side dish in minutes. Play with this recipe—there are tons of possibilities. For a pretty presentation, butter a ramekin and pack the couscous mixture in, then invert onto a dinner plate to serve.

2½ cups vegetable broth

1 cinnamon stick

¼ cup chopped dried cherries

¼ cup chopped dried apricots

2 tablespoons butter

salt and freshly ground black pepper

1 (17.6-ounce) box Trader Joe's Whole Wheat Couscous

VEGETARIAN

Place the chicken broth, cinnamon stick, dried cherries, dried apricots, butter, and a pinch of salt in a medium saucepan over high heat and bring to a boil. Stir in the couscous, cover, and remove from the heat. Let stand 5 minutes. Fluff with a fork. Adjust the seasoning with salt and pepper to taste.

Serves: 4 to 6
Prep Time: 10 minutes
Cooking Time: 10 minutes

WHOLE WHEAT COUSCOUS TABBOULEH-STYLE

Authentic tabbouleh is made with bulgur, but Trader Joe's doesn't carry that. I think this version is a good substitute. I'd eat just about any grain prepared this way—the fresh ingredients give such a summery flavor to the good-for-ya grains. I think this dish's flavor improves if it has an hour to meld before serving, but I can rarely wait that long. I like to keep it at room temperature so the tomatoes don't taste starchy. Add some chopped fresh mint if you have any around—yum!

1 cup Trader Joe's Whole Wheat Couscous

1 cup boiling water

juice of 2 lemons

¼ cup olive oil

4 cubes frozen crushed garlic

5 green onions, sliced

2 medium ripe tomatoes, chopped

1 (0.7-ounce) package fresh parsley, chopped

3 Persian cucumbers, chopped

salt and freshly ground black pepper

VEGAN

Place the couscous in a medium heatproof bowl and cover with the boiling water. Stir to combine and cover with plastic wrap. Let stand for 20 minutes. Add the lemon juice, olive oil, garlic, green onions, tomatoes, parsley, and cucumbers, and toss to combine. Season to taste with salt and pepper.

Serves: 4
Prep Time: 10 minutes
Cooking Time: 5 minutes, plus 20 minutes inactive

ISRAELI COUSCOUS

I love Israeli couscous—such roly-poly cuteness. It lends itself to many flavor combinations and makes a great bed for grilled or roasted meats or fish.

½ medium red onion, halved

2 tablespoons butter or olive oil, plus olive oil for brushing

1 (8-ounce) box Trader Joe's Israeli Couscous

1 ¾ cups vegetable broth

¼ cup pitted green olives, whole or coarsely chopped

salt and freshly ground black pepper

VEGAN (IF OIL IS USED INSTEAD OF BUTTER)

Brush the onion halves with olive oil and grill or pan-sear until softened and charred, then coarsely chop. In a medium saucepan over medium-high heat, melt the butter or olive oil. Sauté the couscous until golden, about 3 minutes. Cover the couscous with the vegetable broth and bring to a boil. Reduce the heat to low, cover, and simmer until tender, about 12 minutes. Check to make sure there is enough liquid to keep the couscous from sticking or burning. Stir in the olives and onion. Season to taste with salt and pepper.

Serves: 4
Prep Time: 5 minutes
Cooking Time: 15 minutes

MUJADARA

Easy, quick, satisfying, and vegetarian. Caramelized onions are the key to this delicious side dish. It would be brilliant of TJ's to sell jarred or frozen caramelized onions—they're culinary gold, in my book. But it's easy enough to simmer up a batch, and they freeze well, so make lots. Cook the rice ahead, or use Trader Joe's frozen White Rice Fully Cooked. This dish is sometimes served with a dollop of minted yogurt. Yummy with or without.

3 tablespoons butter

2 onions, thinly sliced

pinch of ground cinnamon

pinch of ground cumin

pinch of ground cloves

3 cups cooked white rice (1 cup uncooked)

1 (17.6-ounce) package Trader Joe's Steamed Ready to Eat Lentils

salt and freshly ground black pepper

VEGETARIAN, GLUTEN-FREE

In a medium sauté pan or skillet over medium heat, melt the butter. Add the onions, stir to coat them evenly with the butter, and sauté until they soften and turn golden, about 20 minutes. Add the cinnamon, cumin, and cloves and sauté until fragrant, 2 to 3 minutes. Add the cooked rice and lentils and warm through, about 2 minutes. Season to taste with salt and pepper.

Serves: 4
Prep Time: 5 minutes
Cooking Time: 25 minutes

FATTOUSH

Similar to Italian panzanella, fattoush is a great way to use up old bread. I toss the pita pieces in at the last minute so they stay crispy, but let the dressing soak in a little more for a softer texture.

4 (6-inch) pitas, cut into bite-size triangles

2 large ripe tomatoes, chopped

1 Persian cucumber, chopped

1 bell pepper, any color, chopped

6 green onions, sliced

2 tablespoons chopped fresh parsley

2 tablespoons chopped fresh mint

2 tablespoons fresh lemon juice

2 tablespoons olive oil

salt and freshly ground black pepper

VEGAN

Preheat the oven to 400°F. Arrange the pita pieces on a rimmed baking sheet and toast until quite crisp, 5 to 7 minutes. Watch carefully so they don't burn. In a medium bowl, toss together the tomatoes, cucumber, bell pepper, green onions, parsley, and mint. Toss with the lemon juice and olive oil. Season to taste with salt and pepper, and let stand at least 20 minutes to meld the flavors. Toss the pita pieces with the salad.

Serves: 4

Prep Time: 15 minutes, plus marinating time

Cooking Time: 10 minutes

IMAM BAYALDI

I could not write an international collection without including this eggplant preparation, if only for the name. It translates as "the priest fainted," and supposedly that's just what happened when the holy man tasted this heavenly combination of flavors. I'll have what he's having.

3 medium Italian eggplants

¼ cup olive oil, divided

1 medium onion, chopped

3 cubes frozen crushed garlic

1 medium red bell pepper, chopped

1 (14.5-ounce) can chopped tomatoes

salt and freshly ground black pepper

juice of 1 lemon

chopped fresh parsley, for garnish

VEGAN, GLUTEN-FREE

Cut the eggplants in half lengthwise. Using a paring knife, inscribe a line around the inside of each half, about ¼ inch from the edge. With a spoon, scoop out the eggplant flesh, leaving a little bit of flesh and the skin intact to form a shell. Set the shells and flesh aside.

In a large sauté pan or skillet, heat 2 tablespoons olive oil over medium-high heat. Sauté the onion until softened and fragrant, 3 to 4 minutes. Add the garlic and sauté until fragrant, 1 to 2 minutes. Add the bell pepper and sauté until softened, 3 to 4 minutes. Add the tomatoes and the eggplant flesh, and sauté until softened, about 5 minutes. Season to taste with salt and pepper. Transfer the mixture to a bowl.

Preheat the oven to 375°F. In the same pan, heat the remaining 2 tablespoons olive oil. Brown each shell briefly on the rim and the bottom, about 3 minutes per side. As the shells are browned, set them in 9 x 13-inch ovenproof baking dishes (two dishes should be enough space to accommodate all the shells). Season the interiors with salt and pepper, and divide the eggplant mixture evenly among the shells. Pour about 1 inch of hot water into each baking dish and cover with foil. Bake until the shells are tender, about 45 minutes. Sprinkle with lemon juice and garnish with parsley.

Serves: 6
Prep Time: 10 minutes
Cooking Time: 1 hour

MUHAMMARA

In Arabic, muhammara *refers to the vibrant brick-red color of the dish. At the cooking school, we call it Red Pepper Walnut Goodness. And it's so gorgeously good for you. If you're lucky enough to have any leftovers, this goodness can be refrigerated and used in a million ways. It's great on pasta, on grilled chicken or fish, with sautéed or steamed green beans, on eggplant . . . it's my new favorite condiment.*

½ cup pomegranate juice

1 cup walnut pieces, toasted

2 cubes frozen crushed garlic

1 (12-ounce) jar roasted red peppers

1 tablespoon balsamic vinegar

1 tablespoon lemon juice

½ teaspoon ground cumin

1 teaspoon honey

salt and freshly ground black pepper

cayenne pepper

pita wedges or bagel chips

VEGETARIAN, GLUTEN-FREE (IF SERVED ON GLUTEN-FREE CRACKERS)

In a small sauté pan or skillet over medium-high heat, bring the pomegranate juice to a boil. Boil the juice until syrupy and about 2 tablespoons remain, 5 to 7 minutes. Set aside. Process the walnut pieces and garlic in a food processor until finely chopped. Add the peppers, vinegar, lemon juice, cumin, honey, and reduced pomegranate juice, and process until well combined and spreadable. Season to taste with salt, pepper, and cayenne, and process to combine. Serve with pita wedges or bagel chips.

Serves: 4 to 6
Prep Time: 10 minutes
Cooking Time: 10 minutes

CHICKEN KABOBS

Serve this tender chicken over salad greens with a simple oil and lemon juice dressing, or in pita pockets with some hummus or a little plain yogurt with some crushed garlic stirred in.

1 medium onion

½ cup olive oil

4 cubes frozen crushed garlic

pinch of saffron, dissolved in about 1 tablespoon hot water

juice of 1 lemon

salt and freshly ground black pepper

2½ to 3 pounds boneless, skinless chicken thighs, cut into 2-inch cubes

Trader Joe's Smooth and Creamy Roasted Red Pepper Hummus

GLUTEN-FREE

In a food processor, chop the onion very finely. Add the olive oil and garlic, and combine. Transfer to a sealable plastic bag, and add the saffron and water, lemon juice, and salt and pepper. Place the chicken pieces in the bag, seal, and shake to coat the chicken with the marinade. Refrigerate for 2 hours, or overnight. Preheat a grill or broiler. Have ready 4 to 6 metal skewers, or bamboo skewers that have been soaked in water for 30 minutes. Remove the chicken from the marinade, discard the marinade, and pat the chicken dry. Skewer 2 or 3 chicken pieces per kabob. Broil or grill the kabobs for 4 minutes, then flip the skewers over and cook until the chicken is no longer pink in the center, about 4 minutes longer. Serve with the hummus.

Serves: 4 to 6

Prep Time: 5 minutes, plus marinating time

Cooking Time: 20 minutes

EGGS POACHED *in* TOMATO SAUCE

A Persian friend once told me that these are a great hangover cure. I'll have them any morning, hungover or not.

2 teaspoons olive oil

2 cubes frozen crushed garlic

1 (14.5-ounce) can diced tomatoes or tomato sauce

handful of spinach (optional)

½ teaspoon dried oregano

4 eggs

salt and freshly ground black pepper

toasted bread or cooked rice

VEGETARIAN, GLUTEN-FREE (IF RICE OR GLUTEN-FREE BREAD IS USED)

In a medium sauté pan or skillet, heat the olive oil over medium-high heat. Sauté the garlic until fragrant, 2 to 3 minutes. Add the tomatoes and the spinach, if using. Crumble the oregano into the sauce. When the tomatoes are warmed through, crack the eggs into the sauce, spacing them evenly around the pan. Season with salt and pepper and cover the pan. Cook until the eggs are the desired firmness, 3 to 6 minutes. Spoon an egg and some sauce onto each piece of toast or onto rice.

Serves: 4

Prep Time: 5 minutes

Cooking Time: 15 minutes

YOGURT CURRIED SHRIMP

Here's a big payoff for very little work! These plump morsels are great with couscous or orzo. The frozen brown rice at TJ's is superquick and easy, too.

1 cup plain yogurt

2 cubes frozen crushed garlic

1 teaspoon curry powder

pinch of red chile pepper flakes

salt and freshly ground black pepper

2 pounds frozen uncooked shrimp, thawed, peeled, and deveined

GLUTEN-FREE

In a large bowl, stir together the yogurt, garlic, curry powder, chile pepper flakes, and a generous pinch each of salt and pepper. Add the shrimp and toss to coat. Cover the bowl with plastic wrap and marinate the shrimp in the refrigerator for 2 hours. Shake off most of the marinade and discard the marinade. Grill or broil until the shrimp until just pink and opaque, about 5 minutes.

Serves: 4 to 6

Prep Time: 5 minutes, plus marinating time

Cooking Time: 5 minutes

DUKKAH CHICKEN

The nut and spice mixture is deliciously unique. The recipe makes more than you will need for the chicken. It's great with pita—dip in olive oil and sprinkle with some of the nutty spice mixture. Whole boneless, skinless chicken breasts will work, too. Just increase the cooking time to about 30 minutes.

1 pound boneless, skinless chicken thighs, cut into strips

1 cup plain yogurt

DUKKAH:

½ cup hazelnuts

1 (2.2-ounce) jar sesame seeds

1 tablespoon ground cumin

1 tablespoon freshly ground black pepper

2 teaspoons red chile pepper flakes

2 teaspoons salt

1 cup Trader Joe's Japanese-Style Panko Bread Crumbs or bread crumbs

In a bowl or sealable plastic bag, marinate the chicken strips in the yogurt in the refrigerator for 1 hour. For the dukkah: In a small sauté pan or skillet over medium heat, toast the hazelnuts until the skins begin to loosen, 4 to 5 minutes. Transfer to a kitchen towel and rub vigorously to remove much of the skin. In the same pan, briefly toast the sesame seeds, about 5 minutes, being careful not to burn them. Combine the hazelnuts, sesame seeds, cumin, black pepper, chile pepper flakes, and salt in a food processor or mortar and pestle and process or pound until the nuts are pulverized and the mixture is well combined but not pasty.

Preheat the oven to 400°F and line a rimmed baking sheet with parchment paper. Combine the panko bread crumbs with ⅓ cup of the dukkah mixture in a pie plate. Remove the chicken from the marinade and discard the marinade. Add the chicken strips, tossing to coat well. Place on the prepared baking sheet. Bake for 15 minutes. Turn the chicken and cook until the panko crumbs are crisp and the chicken is cooked through, about 6 to 8 minutes longer.

Serves: 4

Prep Time: 20 minutes, plus marinating time

Cooking Time: 20 minutes

FESENJAN (CHICKEN *with* POMEGRANATE-WALNUT SAUCE)

Exotic? Sure, but simple to pull off, and the delicious flavors are as beguiling as a tale from the Arabian Nights. *Reducing the pomegranate juice to a syrup makes pomegranate molasses. Make a double batch and store in the fridge (it's great in marinades, vinaigrettes, and sauces).*

1 (16-ounce) bottle pomegranate juice

2 cups walnuts

2½ to 3 pounds bone-in, skin-on chicken breasts or thighs, or a combination

juice of 2 limes

salt and freshly ground black pepper

2 tablespoons butter

2 medium red onions, thinly sliced

½ teaspoon ground cinnamon

2 tablespoons brown sugar

1 to 1½ cups chicken broth

prepared long-grain white or brown rice or Tahdig (page 86), to serve

chopped fresh parsley and pomegranate seeds for garnish

GLUTEN-FREE

In a medium, heavy-bottomed saucepan over medium-high heat, bring the pomegranate juice to a boil. Boil until reduced to about ½ cup with a syrupy consistency, 15 to 20 minutes. Set aside. In a sauté pan or skillet, toast the walnuts over medium heat until fragrant, shaking the pan frequently to prevent burning. Remove from the pan and chop finely. Set aside.

Sprinkle the chicken with the lime juice and let stand for 20 minutes. Season lightly with salt and pepper. In a large sauté pan or skillet, heat the butter over high heat until foamy. Working in batches, so as not to crowd the pan, brown the chicken, skin side down first, until all the chicken is browned on both sides. Transfer the chicken to a platter. Pour off all but 2 tablespoons of the drippings and add the onions. Sprinkle the cinnamon over the onions and sauté until tender, about 5 minutes. Add the reduced pomegranate juice, walnuts, brown sugar, and 1 cup chicken broth. Bring to a boil, reduce the heat to medium-low, and add the chicken. Cover and simmer for 15 minutes. Turn the chicken over. If the sauce is quite thick and beginning to stick to the pan, add another ½ cup chicken broth. Cover and simmer until the chicken is no longer pink in the center, about 20 minutes. Serve over rice and garnish with parsley and pomegranate seeds.

Serves: 4 to 6
Prep Time: 15 minutes
Cooking Time: 1 hour

INVITATION TO INDIA

- LACCHA (TOMATO AND CUCUMBER SALAD)
- CACHUMBER
- PULAO
- POTATO AND CAULIFLOWER BHAJI
- POTATO AND PEA SAMOSAS
- BUTTERNUT SQUASH AND GREEN BEAN CURRY
- CHANA MASALA
- MASALA LENTIL CHICKEN
- CURRY AND YOGURT LAMB CHOPS
- PORK TIKKA MASALA

I love the complex flavor and texture profiles of Indian food. Recipes are developed and handed down within families, so no two curries will be identical. That gives us some room to improvise. While TJ's doesn't carry turmeric or paneer, they do have some tasty simmer sauces and wonderful frozen Indian dishes. So whether you want to curry it up in the kitchen yourself or let the microwave do the heavy lifting, TJ's is a great place to start for a Bombay evening at home.

LACCHA (TOMATO and CUCUMBER SALAD)

The pure simplicity of this lettuce-free salad is a great foil for the deep and complex flavors of Indian cuisine. Serve this in whole wheat flatbread for a fast lunch that's miles from fast food.

1 medium red onion, thinly sliced

2 medium ripe tomatoes, sliced into wedges

4 Persian cucumbers, sliced

juice of 1 lemon

½ teaspoon ground cumin

pinch of cayenne pepper

salt and freshly ground black pepper

VEGAN, GLUTEN-FREE

In a large salad bowl or on a platter, toss together the onion, tomatoes, and cucumbers. Squeeze the lemon juice over the vegetables. In a small bowl, combine the cumin, cayenne, and salt and black pepper to taste. Sprinkle over the salad and toss to distribute.

Serves: 4
Prep Time: 5 minutes
Cooking Time: none

CACHUMBER

Crispy, crunchy, and cooling—the perfect foil to spicy Indian food. You can use this as a base for a lettuce salad, too, or as a sandwich filling.

2 medium ripe tomatoes, seeded and chopped

1 cup chopped onion

¼ cup chopped fresh cilantro

1 to 2 tablespoons minced seeded jalapeño chile, or to taste

juice of 1 lemon

sugar

salt and freshly ground black pepper, to taste

VEGAN, GLUTEN-FREE

Combine the tomatoes, onion, cilantro, jalapeño, and lemon juice in a large bowl. Add sugar, salt, and pepper to taste. Toss and let stand for 30 minutes to let the flavors meld. Taste and adjust the seasonings.

Serves: 4

Prep Time: 5 minutes, plus 30 minutes for flavor melding

Cooking Time: none

PULAO

Remember the boxed rice mix with the catchy song and cable car logo? Well, pulao is where they probably got the idea—toasted rice with all sorts of tasty mix-ins. So pretty and so good. This is great festive vegetarian fare. Add cooked shrimp or chicken for a main dish pulao for carnivores.

4 tablespoons butter

1 medium onion, chopped

2 tablespoons chopped almonds

2 tablespoons golden raisins

2 cups basmati rice

1 teaspoon ground cumin

¼ teaspoon ground ginger

pinch of saffron

1 cinnamon stick

1 cup Trader Joe's Light Coconut Milk

3 cups water

1 cup frozen peas, thawed

salt and freshly ground black pepper

VEGETARIAN, GLUTEN-FREE

In a large saucepan over medium-high heat, melt the butter. Sauté the onion until tender, 4 to 5 minutes. Add the almonds and raisins, and sauté until the almonds are golden, 2 to 3 minutes. Transfer the sautéed mixture to a bowl and set aside. Add the rice, cumin, ginger, saffron, and cinnamon stick, and sauté until fragrant, 3 to 4 minutes. Add the coconut milk and water and bring to a simmer. Reduce the heat to medium-low and cover the pan. Simmer 15 minutes. Remove from the heat but leave the lid on the pan for 5 minutes. Remove the lid and add the peas. Gently fluff the rice and mix in the peas. Season to taste with salt and pepper. Transfer the rice to a platter and garnish with the reserved sautéed mixture.

Serves: 4 to 6

Prep Time: 10 minutes

Cooking Time: 40 minutes

POTATO *and* CAULIFLOWER BHAJI

The term bhaji *sometimes means a fritter, but in this case, it's a bit simpler—basically a simple vegetable curry.*

2 tablespoons olive oil

1 (16-ounce) bag Trader Joe's Teeny Tiny Potatoes

1 teaspoon ground cumin

2 cubes frozen crushed garlic

1 jalapeño chile, minced

curry powder

1 (12-ounce) bag cauliflower florets

1 cup chicken or vegetable broth

salt and freshly ground black pepper

rice or Trader Joe's Tandoori Naan

VEGAN (IF VEGETABLE BROTH IS USED), GLUTEN-FREE (IF SERVED WITHOUT NAAN)

In a large sauté pan or skillet, heat the olive oil over high heat. Sauté the potatoes for 5 minutes. Add the cumin, garlic, jalapeño, and 2 teaspoons curry powder or to taste. Sauté until fragrant, 1 to 2 minutes. Add the cauliflower and sauté to distribute the spices, about 2 minutes. Add the broth and bring to a boil. Lower the heat to medium, cover, and simmer until the vegetables are tender, 10 to 12 minutes. Season to taste with salt and pepper. Serve over hot rice or with naan.

Serves: 4 to 6
Prep Time: 5 minutes
Cooking Time: 20 minutes

POTATO AND PEA SAMOSAS

The TJ's frozen Roasted Potatoes with Roasted Peppers and Onions would be a quick-fix samosa filling if you don't have time to cook the spuds. For fancier samosas, use the fab (and seasonal) frozen Trader Joe's Artisan Puff Pastry instead of pie dough. For extra-pretty, golden samosas, lightly beat an egg in a small bowl and brush it on the crusts just before the samosas go into the oven. The TJ's pie crust can be found in the frozen-food section. You'll need only one crust for this recipe, but you can keep the remaining crust in the freezer for use at a later time.

1 Trader Joe's Gourmet Pie Crust, thawed

½ cup frozen peas, thawed

1 cup finely chopped cooked potatoes

½ (.75-ounce) package fresh cilantro, chopped

½ (15-ounce) jar Trader Joe's Curry Simmer Sauce

salt and freshly ground black pepper

VEGETARIAN

Preheat the oven to 400°F and line a baking sheet with parchment paper. On a floured work surface, roll the dough out slightly and cut into 3-inch circles. You should be able to get about a dozen circles from one round of dough, rerolling once if needed. Put the dough circles on the prepared baking sheet, and refrigerate while you prepare the filling. In a medium bowl, combine the peas, potatoes, cilantro, and simmer sauce. Adjust the seasoning to taste with salt, pepper, and additional cilantro. Top each dough circle with a scant tablespoon of the filling, keeping the edges of the circles clean. Don't overfill or the samosas will burst open in the oven. Bring the edges of the circles together, forming half-moons of dough. Pinch the edges with your fingers or a fork to seal. Bake until golden, 15 to 18 minutes. Serve warm.

Makes: 12
Prep Time: 20 minutes
Cooking Time: 20 minutes

BUTTERNUT SQUASH *and* GREEN BEAN CURRY

The colors of this dish make me want to dive in—and the aroma is divine.

1 (12-ounce) bag Trader Joe's Cut Butternut Squash

2 cups frozen haricots verts (French green beans)

1 cup Trader Joe's Light Coconut Milk

2 teaspoons curry powder

½ (4-ounce can) Trader Joe's New Mexico Hatch Valley Fire-Roasted Diced Green Chiles

salt and freshly ground black pepper

2 tablespoons chopped cashews, for garnish

VEGAN, GLUTEN-FREE

Place the squash in a medium sauté pan or skillet and add the coconut milk. Bring to a simmer over medium-low heat, and cook until the squash begins to soften, about 12 minutes. Then add the haricots verts and simmer until the vegetables are very tender, 10 to 12 minutes. Stir in the curry powder and chiles, and simmer until fragrant, 2 to 3 minutes longer. Season to taste with salt and pepper. Garnish with chopped cashews.

Serves: 4
Prep Time: 10 minutes
Cooking Time: 25 minutes

CHANA MASALA

These spiced garbanzos in tomato sauce make a terrific main or side dish. Scoop up with some TJ's frozen naan or serve on top of rice.

2 teaspoons grapeseed oil

½ medium onion, chopped

2 cubes frozen crushed garlic

2 teaspoons curry powder

½ teaspoon ground cumin

1 tablespoon minced fresh ginger

1 jalapeño chile, seeded and chopped

1 (15-ounce) can garbanzo beans, drained and rinsed

½ cup tomato sauce

salt and freshly ground black pepper

VEGAN, GLUTEN-FREE

In a medium sauté pan or skillet, heat the grapeseed oil over medium-high heat. Sauté the onion until tender, 3 to 4 minutes. Add the garlic and sauté until fragrant, 1 to 2 minutes. Add the curry powder, cumin, ginger, and jalapeño, and sauté until fragrant, 1 to 2 minutes. Add the garbanzo beans and tomato sauce, and simmer until warmed through, about 3 minutes. Season to taste with salt and pepper.

Serves: 2 as main dish, 4 as side

Prep Time: 10 minutes

Cooking Time: 15 minutes

MASALA LENTIL CHICKEN

TJ's Masala Lentil Dip is found with the refrigerated dips and hummus. Of course it's delish with crudités or crackers, but the flavor lends itself nicely to a sauce for simmering. The sauce is slurpable, so serve on top of saffron rice, couscous, or mashed potatoes, to savor every bit.

6 bone-in, skin-on chicken thighs

salt and freshly ground black pepper

½ teaspoon curry powder

1 tablespoon olive oil

1 medium red onion, sliced

1 (7-ounce) container Trader Joe's Masala Lentil Dip

¾ cup chicken broth or water

Season the chicken with salt, pepper, and curry powder. In a medium sauté pan or skillet, heat the olive oil over high heat. Brown the chicken on both sides, about 4 minutes per side. Transfer the chicken to a plate and set aside. Pour off all but 2 tablespoons of the oil. Sauté the onion until softened, 3 to 4 minutes. Add the lentil dip and the chicken broth or water, and stir to combine. Place the chicken on top of the sauce. Cover the pan and simmer for 10 minutes. Remove the lid, stir the sauce, and turn the chicken over. Simmer, covered, until the chicken is no longer pink in the center, about 10 minutes longer.

Serves: 4 to 6
Prep Time: 5 minutes
Cooking Time: 45 minutes

CURRY *and* YOGURT LAMB CHOPS

The vibrant color of the curry powder is so gorgeous. You know we eat with our eyes before our taste buds, and this one is a feast for both.

½ cup plain yogurt

1½ tablespoons curry powder

2 tablespoons tomato paste

2 cubes frozen crushed garlic

4 lamb shoulder or loin chops

salt and pepper

cooked basmati rice

In a small bowl, stir together the yogurt, curry powder, tomato paste, and garlic. Season the lamb with salt and pepper, and slather the yogurt mixture over the chops. Marinate 20 minutes. Remove the lamb from the marinade and discard the marinade. Heat a grill, grill pan, or broiler to medium-high. Cook the lamb 4 minutes on the first side, turn, and cook 4 minutes on the second side for medium-rare. Serve over a bed of basmati rice.

Serves: 4

Prep Time: 5 minutes

Cooking Time: 10 minutes

PORK TIKKA MASALA

Tikka means bits and pieces, and masala *means spice mixture. Rich and flavorful, these spicy bits can be made with pork or chicken with equally delicious results. Serve over white or brown rice, or with some of the fab frozen TJ's Garlic Naan.*

MARINADE:

2 cups plain low-fat yogurt

juice of 1 lemon

1 teaspoon ground cumin

2 teaspoons ground cinnamon

1 to 2 teaspoons cayenne pepper

2 tablespoons minced fresh ginger

salt and pepper

1 (1 to 1½-pound) pork tenderloin, cut into bite-size pieces

SAUCE:

1 tablespoon butter

4 cubes frozen crushed garlic

1 jalapeño chile, minced

1 teaspoon ground cumin

1 tablespoon paprika

1 (15-ounce) can tomato sauce

½ cup half-and-half or cream

salt and pepper

1 (.75-ounce) package fresh cilantro, chopped

For the marinade: In a large bowl, combine the yogurt, lemon juice, cumin, cinnamon, cayenne, ginger, and salt and pepper to taste. Add the pork and marinate, refrigerated, for at least 2 hours or overnight. Remove the pork from the marinade, discard the marinade, and pat the pork dry. Heat a grill, grill pan, or broiler to medium-high and cook the pork until browned on the edges and nearly cooked through, 5 to 8 minutes. The cooking time will depend on the size of the pieces and the heat of the cooking method.

For the sauce: In a medium saucepan over medium-high heat, melt the butter. Add the garlic and jalapeño, and sauté until fragrant, 2 to 3 minutes. Add the cumin, paprika, and tomato sauce. Bring to a boil. Reduce the heat to low and simmer for 5 minutes. Add the half-and-half or cream, and simmer until slightly thickened, about 5 minutes.

Add the pork cubes and simmer until cooked through, about 2 minutes. Season to taste with salt and pepper. Garnish with cilantro.

Serves: 4

Prep Time: 20 minutes, plus marinating time

Cooking Time: 30 minutes

ASIAN INFLUENCE

- FAST FAUX PHO
- POTSTICKER SOUP
- THAI BEEF SALAD
- WASABI SLAW
- HOT AND SOUR SHRIMP SOUP
- LETTUCE WRAP MEATBALLS
- CRAB FRIED RICE
- NEGIMA
- BANH MI
- LARB
- STIR-FRIED PORK AND VEGETABLES WITH SATAY SAUCE
- GENERAL TSAO PORK
- TONKATSU
- THAI GREEN CURRY WITH CHICKEN AND RICE

Asian dishes are a feast for the senses—the vibrant colors of the vegetables and herbs, the pleasing appearance of tangled peppers and onions, the tantalizing aroma and sound of sizzling garlic and soy sauce, and of course, the explosion of flavors that a great balance of salty, sweet, spicy, and sour bring to the palate. Not to mention that they are generally quick-cook recipes, especially if you let TJ's take care of most of the work for you. Precut veggies and great simmer and dipping sauces really cut down the prep time and increase the enjoyment time!

FAST FAUX PHO

I'm lucky enough to live close to several great Vietnamese pho *shops, so when I have a craving (or a cold), I have options. The broth they serve is rich and deeply flavored from hours of simmering bones and aromatics. This is a quick, homemade version of those complexly flavored bowls of goodness. TJ's doesn't carry star anise, which brings a traditional note of exotic spice to the soup. If you happen to have one or two in your spice cupboard, toss them into the simmering broth.*

4 cups beef broth

1 cinnamon stick

pinch of ground cloves

2 (¼-inch) slices fresh ginger

1 tablespoon soy sauce

1 teaspoon brown sugar

handful of thin rice noodles

½ pound Trader Joe's Very Thinly Sliced Sirloin

1 medium yellow onion, thinly sliced

1 cup chopped fresh herbs, like basil, cilantro, or mint, or a combination

4 green onions, sliced

juice of 2 fresh limes

1 jalapeño chile, minced

In a medium saucepan, combine the beef broth, cinnamon stick, cloves, ginger, soy sauce, and brown sugar. Bring to a boil over high heat. Reduce the heat to medium-low, and simmer for 30 minutes. Strain the broth, discard the solids, and return the broth to a simmer in the saucepan. This can be done hours or days ahead. Refrigerate the broth until ready to use, then reheat.

Place the rice noodles in a large heatproof bowl and cover with very hot water. Let stand until softened, about 15 minutes.

Add the beef to the hot broth, and simmer until it loses its raw appearance, about 4 minutes. Drain the rice noodles and add to the broth. At this point, you can add the onion, herbs, green onions, lime juice, and jalapeño, or serve them in separate small bowls for each person to garnish their pho according to their taste.

Serves: 4
Prep Time: 10 minutes
Cooking Time: 45 minutes

POTSTICKER SOUP

Couldn't be simpler to put together, but the results are so, so good. This is one of the recipes I hear about from readers who've made it so many times they know it by heart.

4 cups chicken or vegetable broth

1 tablespoon seasoned rice vinegar

1 tablespoon soy sauce

2 cubes frozen crushed garlic

½ (16-ounce) package frozen Trader Joe's Chicken or Vegetable Gyoza Potstickers (about 12)

1 (20-ounce) bag Trader Joe's Stir Fry Vegetables

½ cup shredded carrots

4 green onions, thinly sliced

2 teaspoons toasted sesame oil

VEGETARIAN (IF VEGETABLE BROTH AND VEGETARIAN POTSTICKERS ARE USED)

In a medium saucepan, combine the broth, rice vinegar, soy sauce, and garlic. Bring to a boil over high heat. Add the potstickers and return to a boil. Lower the heat to medium and simmer for 4 minutes. Add the stir-fry vegetables and carrots and simmer until the vegetables are tender and the potstickers are cooked through, about 3 minutes. Garnish with green onions and a drizzle of sesame oil.

Serves: 4 to 6
Prep Time: 5 minutes
Cooking Time: 15 minutes

CRAB FRIED RICE

If you put this in a Chinese take-out carton, no one will suspect it's not the work of a restaurant wokmaster. I think the canned crabmeat (found in the refrigerated section) has much better flavor than the shelf-stable kind. The lump crab is terrific but more expensive than the claw meat, which I find to be just fine for this recipe. And believe it or not, day-old cooked rice is actually best in this recipe.

2 tablespoons grapeseed oil

6 cubes frozen crushed garlic

4 cups cooked long-grain white rice, at room temperature

3 eggs

2 tablespoons soy sauce

½ cup frozen peas

½ cup shredded carrots

2 teaspoons toasted sesame oil

½ pound canned claw crabmeat

Heat the grapeseed oil in a large sauté pan or skillet over medium-high heat. Sauté the garlic until fragrant, 1 to 2 minutes. Add the rice and sauté until heated through. In a small bowl, lightly beat the eggs together, then add them to the pan, stirring to incorporate. Add the soy sauce, peas, and carrots, and stir to combine. Add the sesame oil and crabmeat, and stir to combine. Adjust the seasoning with additional soy sauce and sesame oil.

Serves: 4

Prep Time: 5 minutes

Cooking Time: 10 minutes

NEGIMA

Negi *in Japanese means "green onion." These smoky, richly flavored morsels combine green onions with rare, thinly sliced beef. You could use asparagus instead of, or in addition to, the green onions, but I suppose you'd have to learn how to say "asparagus" in Japanese.*

¼ cup soy sauce

1 tablespoon seasoned rice vinegar

1 teaspoon minced fresh ginger

1 cube frozen crushed garlic

1 teaspoon honey or agave syrup

12 green onions

½ pound sirloin or rib-eye steak, thinly sliced

In a small bowl, stir together the soy sauce, rice vinegar, ginger, garlic, and honey or agave syrup. In a medium bowl or sealable plastic bag, marinate the green onions and steak strips at least 30 minutes. Preheat the broiler and broiler pan. Remove the roots of the green onions and trim each one to 4 inches long. Wrap a steak strip around each green onion, securing it with a toothpick if needed. Carefully arrange the rolls on the hot broiler pan and broil until the meat is cooked rare, 3 to 4 minutes.

Serves: 4

Prep Time: 10 minutes, plus marinating time

Cooking Time: 5 minutes

BANH MI

Sweet, crunchy, spicy, buttery, and meaty, all on a baguette? Sign me up for that. And by "that" I mean banh mi, *arguably the sandwich perfected. These Vietnamese wonder bundles are great at a picnic, or while standing over the kitchen sink. Tomato slices are also tasty on a* bahn mi, *but only if they are gorgeous and ripe. You might have leftover carrots—they are great in salads.*

½ (10-ounce) bag shredded carrots

1 cup water

½ cup seasoned rice vinegar

½ cup sugar

2 tablespoons salt

generous pinch of red chile pepper flakes

2 Trader Joe's French Demi Baguettes, or 1 regular baguette

2 tablespoons butter, at room temperature

½ (7-ounce) container Trader Joe's Truffle Mousse Pâté (Chicken)

4 slices ham or roasted pork

4 slices roasted turkey

1 to 2 jalapeño chiles, seeded and very thinly sliced

handful of cilantro sprigs

To quick-pickle the carrots, place them in a heatproof bowl. In a small saucepan, combine the water, rice vinegar, sugar, and salt over high heat. Bring to a boil and cook until the sugar dissolves. Cool to room temperature. Add the chile pepper flakes and the carrots, and toss to combine. Let stand for at least 30 minutes. Drain.

Split the baguettes lengthwise and spread the butter over the cut sides of each roll. Spread or thinly slice the pâté over the buttered side of 2 baguette slices. Arrange the ham and turkey on top and tuck in the jalapeño and cilantro. Add some pickled carrots to each sandwich. Add the baguette tops and serve the sandwiches.

Serves: 2 as a meal, 4 as a snack
Prep Time: 15 minutes
Cooking Time: none

LARB

*Larb might be the original lettuce wrap. Kind of saucy, a little spicy—
this stuff could be the mother of Sloppy Joes. The fresh citrus juice
gives the meat such bright flavor, and the fresh herbs are gorgeous and
delicious.*

grated zest and juice of 2 limes

grated zest of 1 lemon and juice
of ½ lemon

2 tablespoons soy sauce

1 teaspoon toasted sesame oil

1 tablespoon brown sugar

1 jalapeño chile, finely chopped

pinch of red chile pepper flakes

2 teaspoons grapeseed oil

1 shallot, finely chopped

1 pound ground white plus dark
meat turkey

¼ cup coarsely chopped fresh
mint

¼ cup coarsely chopped fresh
basil

4 green onions, coarsely chopped

romaine or butter lettuce leaves,
for scooping

salt

In a medium bowl, whisk together the lime zest and
juice, lemon zest and juice, soy sauce, sesame oil,
brown sugar, jalapeño, and chile pepper flakes. Set
aside. In a medium sauté pan or skillet, heat the
grapeseed oil over medium-high heat. Sauté the shallot
until just tender, 2 to 3 minutes. Add the ground turkey
and sauté until cooked through and no longer pink,
about 7 minutes. Add the citrus and soy sauce mixture
and combine. Add the chopped mint, basil, and green
onions and toss. Adjust the seasoning with salt or
additional soy sauce. Serve with lettuce leaves for
scooping the larb.

Serves: 4
Prep Time: 15 minutes
Cooking Time: 15 minutes

I prefer to use ground turkey with some dark meat included,
rather than 100 percent breast meat. That little bit of fat helps
keep the turkey from drying out and gives it great flavor. This is
also delicious with ground beef or pork in addition to, or instead
of, the turkey.

STIR-FRIED PORK *and* VEGETABLES WITH SATAY SAUCE

Vibrant colors and veggies galore make this dish a winner. You can have it on the table faster than getting dinner delivery, and it's much more economical. Substitute sherry or white wine for the chicken broth if you feel so inclined. Of course, you could also use cubed chicken thighs or breasts or firm tofu in place of the pork. This dish is great tossed with cooked pasta, or served atop brown or white rice.

1 to 2 tablespoons grapeseed oil

1 (1-pound) pork tenderloin cut into thin strips

1 (18-ounce) package Trader Joe's Asian Stir Fry Vegetables

½ cup chicken broth

1 (9-ounce) jar Trader Joe's Satay Peanut Sauce

salt and freshly ground black pepper

red chile pepper flakes

In a large sauté pan or skillet, heat 1 tablespoon grapeseed oil over high heat. Sauté the pork until just cooked through, 4 to 6 minutes. Remove from the pan with a slotted spoon. In the same pan, sauté the vegetables for 4 minutes, adding a little more oil if necessary to keep them from sticking, then add the chicken broth. Simmer until the vegetables are just tender. Add the pork and any accumulated juices back to the pan, and pour in the satay sauce. Stir to heat through. Season to taste with salt, pepper, and chile pepper flakes.

Serves: 4
Prep Time: 5 minutes
Cooking Time: 20 minutes

GENERAL TSAO PORK

Oh, that General Tsao sauce—so sweetly spicy and delicious. Great as a dipping sauce for pot stickers, as a glaze for grilled meats, or even in a vinaigrette for an Asian salad. Definitely on the hoardable list!

2 teaspoons olive oil

3 cubes frozen crushed garlic

1 (1½-pound) pork tenderloin, cut into ½-inch-thick medallions (rounds)

½ cup Trader Ming's General Tsao Stir Fry Sauce

1½ cups chicken broth

handful of haricots verts (French green beans)

½ (13.2-ounce) bag Trader Joe's Rice Sticks (Thai pasta)

½ (10-ounce) bag shredded carrots

In a large sauté pan or skillet, heat the olive oil over medium-high heat. Sauté the garlic until aromatic, 1 to 2 minutes. Add the pork and sauté until it begins to brown, 4 to 5 minutes. Add the sauce and chicken broth, and bring to a boil. Reduce the heat to low and simmer until the pork is no longer pink, 10 to 12 minutes. While the pork cooks, bring a saucepan of water to a boil and add the green beans and rice sticks. Boil until both are tender, about 5 minutes. Drain the noodles and beans, and toss in the shredded carrots. Top the noodles with the pork and sauce and serve.

Serves: 4

Prep Time: 10 minutes

Cooking Time: 20 minutes

• •

Trader Joe's Rice Sticks can be found with the grains and pad Thai. They're not always available, so stock up when you see them. In a pinch, spaghetti or linguine will work instead, but increase the cooking time to 8 minutes and add the green beans 3 minutes after adding the pasta to the water.

• •

TONKATSU

Tonkatsu is usually deep-fried, but pan-frying the pork makes it a little more practical for the home cook. If you're into deep-frying at home, by all means go for it. Traditionally, the crispy, tender morsels are served with a mound of shredded cabbage. I like to throw in a handful of shredded carrots, and maybe a drizzle of soy dressing. If you have time, set the breaded medallions on a wire rack and refrigerate them for a couple hours. This will help the breading hold onto the meat better.

1 (1-pound) pork tenderloin, cut into ½-inch-thick medallions (rounds)

1 cup flour

1 (12.35-ounce) bottle Trader Ming's General Tsao Stir Fry Sauce

½ (7-ounce) bag Trader Joe's Japanese-Style Panko Bread Crumbs

½ cup grapeseed oil

Flatten the pork medallions with the palm of your hand or a meat mallet to about ¼-inch thickness. Fill a shallow bowl with the flour. Fill a second shallow bowl with about half the sauce, and a third bowl with half the panko crumbs. Dip a medallion into the flour, coating both sides. Shake off the excess flour and dip the medallion into the sauce, then into the panko crumbs, patting to coat well on both sides. Repeat until all the medallions are breaded.

In a medium sauté pan or skillet, heat the grapeseed oil over medium-high heat until it shimmers. To test the heat, place the handle of a wooden spoon into the oil. Bubbles should form around the handle within a few seconds. Fry two or three medallions at a time until golden on both sides, 2 to 3 minutes per side. Set on a paper towel to drain, and repeat until all the medallions are fried. Serve the pork with the remaining sauce.

Serves: 4
Prep Time: 15 minutes
Cooking Time: 15 minutes

THAI GREEN CURRY *with* CHICKEN *and* RICE

A super one-dish meal that requires very little prep, this will have the house smelling amazing as soon as it starts to simmer.

2 tablespoons grapeseed oil

1 medium red onion, thinly sliced

3 cubes frozen crushed garlic

1½ pounds boneless skinless chicken thighs

1 (12-ounce) jar Trader Joe's Thai Green Curry Simmer Sauce

1 (14-ounce) can Trader Joe's Light Coconut Milk

1 cup water or chicken broth

½ (12-ounce) bag fresh haricots verts (French green beans)

1 (1-pint) package Trader Joe's Minisweet Peppers, cut into rings

1½ cups uncooked jasmine or basmati rice

1 cup shredded carrots

salt and freshly ground black pepper

In a large sauté pan or skillet, heat the grapeseed oil over high heat. Sauté the onion until softened, about 3 minutes. Add the garlic and sauté until fragrant, about 2 minutes. Add the chicken, curry simmer sauce, coconut milk, water or broth, haricots verts, and mini bell peppers. Bring the liquid to a boil, reduce the heat to low, and stir in the rice. Cover and simmer for 20 minutes, uncovering twice to stir. Remove the lid, stir in the carrots, and season to taste with salt and pepper. Check that the chicken is no longer pink n the center, taste the rice for doneness, and simmer for a few more minutes if not tender.

Serves: 4 to 6
Prep Time: 5 minutes
Cooking Time: 30 minutes

ISLAND FLAVORS

- BLACK BEAN SALAD
- MANGO-LANGO SALAD
- GRILLED SWORDFISH WITH MANGO SALSA
- PAPAS APLASTADAS (SMASHED POTATOES)
- MEDIANOCHE
- MOJO CRIOLLO
- CUBAN GARLIC CHICKEN
- HULI-HULI CHICKEN
- SHORTCUT VACA FRITA
- MAUI BEEF ON COCONUT RICE WITH MACADAMIA NUTS AND BASIL
- FLANK STEAK WITH DOG SAUCE
- TROPICAL TENDERLOIN

You'll find a little bit of Cuban verve, a little Jamaican groove, some Hawaiian influence, and a whole lotta flavor under this Island umbrella! If it's got a mango or a mojo, you'll find it here. Get your island groove on, take your shoes off, and channel some of those laid-back tropical rays while you cook.

BLACK BEAN SALAD

A bit of Cuban flare in a great picnic or barbecue side dish. The cumin and cilantro bring some tropical smoke and spiciness, and the sweet-tart vinegar adds a mojo vibe to the dressing. Toss in chopped mango or avocado if you've got some.

2 (15-ounce) cans black beans, drained and rinsed

3 ribs celery, chopped

1 medium red onion, chopped

1 (¾-ounce) package fresh cilantro, chopped

1 teaspoon ground cumin

¼ teaspoon red chile pepper flakes

2 tablespoons Trader Joe's Orange Muscat Champagne Vinegar or red wine vinegar

1 teaspoon Dijon mustard

½ cup olive oil

salt and freshly ground black pepper

VEGAN, GLUTEN-FREE

In a medium bowl, combine the black beans, celery, onion, and cilantro. In a small bowl, combine the cumin, chile pepper flakes, vinegar, and mustard, then whisk in the olive oil. Toss the bean mixture with the dressing. Season to taste with salt and pepper.

Serves: 4 to 6
Prep Time: 15 minutes
Cooking Time: none

MANGO-LANGO SALAD

Such a gorgeous summer lunch. The soft textures of the avocado and mango reveal very different flavors on the fork. One buttery, one brightly acidic—a dynamic duo, for sure. The pretty pink langoustines add visual appeal. Oh, and they are so tasty! Nectarines or peaches would be terrific stand-ins for mango in this salad (but they don't rhyme with lango*).*

1 (5-ounce) bag Trader Joe's Baby Spring Mix

1 ripe avocado, cubed

1 ripe mango, cubed

2 Persian cucumbers, sliced

1 tablespoon butter

1 tablespoon olive oil

1 (12-ounce) bag frozen langoustine tails, thawed

salt and freshly ground black pepper

pinch of cayenne pepper

1 tablespoon Trader Joe's Champagne Muscat Orange Vinegar

GLUTEN-FREE

Arrange the greens on a platter. Scatter the avocado, mango, and cucumbers over the salad. In a medium sauté pan or skillet, heat the butter and olive oil over medium-high heat. Sauté the langoustine tails until pink and hot, 3 to 4 minutes. Season with a little salt, black pepper, and cayenne. Remove the langos from the pan with a slotted spoon and place on top of the salad. Whisk the vinegar into the pan drippings. Adjust the seasoning with salt and pepper, and drizzle over the salad.

Serves: 4
Prep Time: 10 minutes
Cooking Time: 5 minutes

GRILLED SWORDFISH *with* MANGO SALSA

This salsa is great with grilled chicken or pork as well—or just chips!

MANGO SALSA:

1 cup chopped fresh mango

1 jalapeño chile, seeded and minced

¼ cup chopped red onion

¼ cup chopped fresh cilantro

juice of 1 lime, or more as needed

salt and freshly ground black pepper

pinch of cayenne pepper

1½ pounds frozen swordfish or any firm-fleshed fish, thawed

2 teaspoons grapeseed oil

GLUTEN-FREE

For the salsa: Combine the mango, jalapeño, onion, cilantro, and lime juice in a medium bowl. Let stand at least 30 minutes to meld the flavors. Adjust the seasoning as needed with salt, pepper, and more lime juice. Use a pinch of cayenne if you want more heat than the jalapeño provides.

Season the fish with a little salt and pepper. In a medium sauté pan or skillet, heat the grapeseed oil over medium-high heat. Cook the fish until a knife blade inserted into the center comes out warm to the touch, 2 to 3 minutes per side. Serve with the salsa.

Serves: 4 to 6

Prep Time: 10 minutes, plus marinating time

Cooking Time: 10 minutes

PAPAS APLASTADAS (SMASHED POTATOES)

These are just plain fun to make, as well as delicioso! *Put guests or kids to work gently flattening the spuds—it's fun and a great conversation starter.*

2 pounds red or white boiling potatoes, or a combination

3 strips bacon, chopped

1 cup chopped green, red, or yellow bell peppers, or a mixture

3 cubes frozen crushed garlic

1 to 2 tablespoons olive oil (optional)

1 teaspoon salt

¼ teaspoon freshly ground black pepper

½ teaspoon ground cumin

½ cup chopped green onions

1 cup shredded Jack or cheddar cheese, or a blend

GLUTEN-FREE

Steam or boil the potatoes until tender, 15 to 20 minutes. Drain the potatoes and arrange in a single layer on a rimmed baking sheet to cool slightly. With your hands, gently press the potatoes until nearly flat. Cook the bacon over medium-high heat in a sauté pan or skillet until crisp, about 5 minutes. Crumble the bacon over the potatoes. In the pan with the bacon fat, sauté the bell peppers over medium-high heat until tender, about 5 minutes. Add the garlic and sauté until fragrant, 1 to 2 minutes longer. Scatter the vegetables evenly over the potatoes. If using the olive oil, sprinkle it over the potatoes. In a small bowl, combine the salt, pepper, and cumin, and season the potatoes. Top with the green onions and cheese. Preheat the oven's broiler and position a rack at least 4 inches from the heat source. Cook the potatoes until the cheese is melted and just beginning to brown, about 5 minutes. Watch it carefully, because you'll cry if the potatoes burn!

Serves: 6 to 8
Prep Time: 10 minutes
Cooking Time: 35 minutes

MEDIANOCHE

This is a perfect Cuban combination of tangy pickle, sweet and savory pork, cheesy goodness, and crisped bread.

1 (12.6-ounce) package panini rolls

2 tablespoons Trader Joe's Deli Style Spicy Brown Mustard, more or less

2 tablespoons organic mayonnaise, more or less

4 slices Swiss or Havarti cheese

4 pickle strips

4 slices Black Forest Healthy Smoked Ham

melted butter

Heat a griddle, grill pan, or panini maker. Split each roll lengthwise and spread lightly with mustard and mayonnaise. For each sandwich, place a slice of cheese on one side of the roll and a pickle strip on the other side. Top the pickle with a slice of ham and close the sandwich. Brush both sides of each roll with a little melted butter and grill the sandwiches on each side, pressing down firmly or weighting, until crisp and flattened, about 5 minutes.

Serves: 4

Prep Time: 10 minutes

Cooking Time: 5 minutes per sandwich

MOJO CRIOLLO

If I could use only one sauce or marinade for the rest of my cooking days, I might pick this one. So versatile, so zingy-fresh, so full of sabor. Use it to marinate chicken or pork, brush on grilled vegetables, or drizzle on steamed rice.

¼ cup olive oil

1 medium onion, finely chopped

6 cubes frozen crushed garlic

½ teaspoon ground cumin

1 (.75-ounce) package fresh parsley, chopped

1 (.75-ounce) package fresh cilantro, chopped

1 cup fresh orange juice

juice of 4 limes

salt and freshly ground black pepper

VEGAN (IF SERVED ON RICE OR VEGETABLES), GLUTEN-FREE

In a medium sauté pan or skillet, heat the olive oil over medium-high heat. Sauté the onion until softened, 3 to 4 minutes. Add the garlic and cumin, and sauté 1 minute. Scrape the mixture into a heatproof bowl and let cool for 5 minutes. Add the parsley, cilantro, orange juice, and lime juice. Season to taste with salt and pepper.

Makes: about 1½ cups
Prep Time: 10 minutes
Cooking Time: 5 minutes

CUBAN GARLIC CHICKEN

Yeah, it's a lot of garlic, but Cuban flavors are big and bold. No one will be able to resist the aroma of this juicy goodness.

10 cubes frozen crushed garlic

2 teaspoons salt

2 medium white onions, cut into eighths

½ cup white wine

¼ cup olive oil

1 tablespoon white vinegar

3 pounds bone-in, skin-on chicken pieces, or 1 (4-pound) chicken, butterflied

juice of 1 lime

freshly ground black pepper

1 teaspoon ground cumin

GLUTEN-FREE

Stir the garlic with the salt to make a paste. Divide the paste in half. In a food processor or blender, puree the onion, half the garlic paste, the white wine, olive oil, and vinegar. Place the chicken in a large sealable plastic bag, or nonreactive container with a cover, and pour the marinade over the chicken, turning to coat well. Marinate in the refrigerator for at least 3 hours or overnight. Preheat the oven to 400°F. (Use the oven's convection setting, if you have it, for crisper skin. Convection also shortens the cooking time.) Remove the chicken from the marinade, pat dry with paper towels, and discard the marinade. Carefully loosen the skin and rub some of the remaining garlic paste under the skin. Rub the remainder over the top of the skin. Place the chicken in a single layer on a rimmed baking sheet or in a shallow baking dish. Sprinkle with lime juice, pepper, and cumin. Roast until the skin is crisp and the chicken is no longer pink in the center, 35 to 45 minutes.

Serves: 6
Prep Time: 15 minutes, plus marinating time
Cooking Time: 45 minutes

HULI-HULI CHICKEN

Authentic Hawaiian huli-huli *chicken requires rotisserie grilling over* kiawe *wood—a bit hard to find on the mainland. Mesquite is a fine substitute, and TJ's carries it in summer. Since we're all about improvisation with TJ's items, you can use mesquite wood on a charcoal grill or a gas grill, or even roast the chicken in your oven— whatever works for you! Traditional* huli-huli *calls for a butterflied chicken (backbone removed). A pair of poultry shears makes this a pretty easy process, but if I'm doing this on the rotisserie, I find it harder to balance the bird when it's split this way. So I usually grill it on the grates, or skip the grill and oven it up!*

1 (4 to 5-pound) chicken or cut-up chicken pieces

½ cup soy sauce

¼ cup freshly squeezed lime juice

¼ cup honey

2 tablespoons brown sugar

1 tablespoon olive oil

2 cubes frozen crushed garlic

2 tablespoons ketchup

1 tablespoon minced fresh ginger

several dashes Trader Joe's Chili Pepper Hot Sauce or Jalapeño Pepper Hot Sauce

1 teaspoon toasted sesame oil

salt and freshly ground black pepper

Combine all the ingredients in a large sealable plastic bag or a nonreactive container with a lid. Marinate the chicken in the refrigerator for at least 30 minutes or up to overnight. Preheat a grill to medium-high or the oven to 375°F. Grill the chicken (on a rotisserie or on the grates), turning occasionally and basting frequently, until the internal temperature reaches 160°F, about 25 minutes, or about 40 minutes in the oven.

Serves: 6

Prep Time: 15 minutes, plus marinating time

Cooking Time: 25 minutes (on the grill) or 40 minutes (in the oven)

SHORTCUT VACA FRITA

The credit for this idea goes to the very entertaining Three Guys from Miami. They've written several unconventional (and hilarious) cookbooks celebrating their love of Cuban cuisine. I love the idea of using leftover roast beef for the dish, but it's also great with strips of cooked flank steak. This is terrific on top of rice and black beans or folded into tortillas. For a breakfast you won't forget, scramble or soft-cook a couple eggs in the pan once the meat is hot and crisped. The precooked pot roast can be found in TJ's refrigerated section.

1 (16-ounce) package precooked Trader Joe's Traditional Pot Roast

2 tablespoons dry sherry

1 teaspoon ground cumin

1 teaspoon dried oregano

¼ cup olive oil

2 medium onions, thinly sliced

4 cubes frozen crushed garlic

2 bell peppers, cut into strips

salt and freshly ground black pepper

juice of 1 lime

Microwave the beef on high power until warm, 2 to 3 minutes. Using your fingers, or two forks, pull the meat apart into shreds. Sprinkle the meat with the sherry, cumin, and oregano, tossing to distribute evenly. In a large sauté pan or skillet, heat the olive oil over medium-high heat. Sauté the onions until softened, 4 to 5 minutes. Add the garlic and sauté until aromatic, about 2 minutes. Add the bell peppers and sauté until softened, 3 to 4 minutes. Add the meat and sauté until crisped and warmed through, about 10 minutes. Season with salt, pepper, and lime juice.

Serves: 4
Prep Time: 10 minutes
Cooking Time: 25 minutes

MAUI BEEF *on* COCONUT RICE *with* MACADAMIA NUTS *and* BASIL

Practically a meal in a bowl, the subtle coconut flavor of the rice is terrific with the tender beef and bright punch of basil. Add the pretty, yummy mango and you've got a winning dinner for family or guests. If you love the flavor of coconut, increase the amount of coconut milk to 1½ cups and use only ½ cup of water to make the rice. Also, in place of the jasmine or basmati rice, you can use frozen Trader Joe's Thai Jasmine Rice and omit the water or broth.

1 cup Trader Joe's Light Coconut Milk

1 cup water, or vegetable or chicken broth

1 cup jasmine or basmati rice

salt

¼ cup macadamia nuts, chopped

handful of fresh basil leaves, sliced into chiffonade (see page 186)

1 to 1½ pounds Trader Joe's Hawaiian Style Maui Beef Boneless Short Ribs

½ fresh mango, sliced, or ½ (12-ounce) package sliced fresh mango, for garnish

In a medium saucepan over high heat, bring the coconut milk and water or broth to a boil. Stir in the rice and bring the liquid back to a boil. Reduce the heat to very low, cover, and cook for 15 minutes. Remove from the heat, leaving the lid on, and let stand 5 minutes. Remove the lid, fluff the rice, and season with a little salt. Stir in the nuts. Just before serving, sprinkle with the basil. Grill or broil the short ribs until the desired degree of doneness, 3 to 5 minutes per side. Serve the beef on top of the rice, garnished with mango slices.

Serves: 4 to 6
Prep Time: 10 minutes
Cooking Time: 25 minutes

FLANK STEAK WITH DOG SAUCE

Don't freak—no dogs are harmed in the making of this sauce. In the West Indies, it's island patois for this spicy sauce that's great on lots of meats. I've heard that the name might derive from the fact that it has a definite bite, or the runny nose its heat may induce! Whatever the reason for the weird name, it's a conversation starter and a delicious condiment.

DOG SAUCE:

6 green onions, trimmed

1 medium shallot, trimmed

1 jalapeño chile, seeded

5 cubes frozen crushed garlic

½ cup fresh parsley leaves

¼ cup fresh cilantro leaves

juice of 1 lime

1 tablespoon cider vinegar

2 tablespoons olive oil

⅓ cup boiling water

salt and freshly ground black pepper

1½ pounds flank steak

GLUTEN-FREE

For the sauce: In a food processor, coarsely chop the green onions, shallot, and jalapeño. Add the garlic, parsley, and cilantro and pulse to chop. Add the lime juice, and cider vinegar, and pulse to combine. Add the olive oil and the boiling water, and pulse to combine again. Season to taste with salt and pepper.

Grill or broil the flank steak until cooked rare, about 3 minutes per side. Serve the steak with the sauce.

Serves: 4 to 6

Prep Time: 10 minutes

Cooking Time: none

TROPICAL TENDERLOIN

One of the most popular dishes at the cooking school, this is frequently the dish I take to a new mom or someone who's been laid up (or laid low). It warms easily, it's tasty, and everyone I take it to asks for the recipe.

1 teaspoon salt

½ teaspoon ground cumin

pinch of cayenne pepper

½ teaspoon ground cinnamon

several grinds black pepper

1 (1 to 1½-pound) pork tenderloin

2 teaspoons olive oil

½ cup brown sugar

3 cubes frozen crushed garlic

several shakes of Trader Joe's Chili Pepper Hot Sauce or Jalapeño Pepper Hot Sauce

GLUTEN-FREE

Place the salt, cumin, cayenne, cinnamon, and black pepper in a sealable plastic bag. Put the pork in the bag with the spices and roll around to coat evenly. This can be done ahead and refrigerated for up to 24 hours. Preheat the oven to 400°F. Heat the olive oil in an ovenproof sauté pan or skillet over high heat. Brown the tenderloin on all sides, about 5 minutes. In a small bowl, combine the brown sugar, garlic, and hot sauce, and cover the top of the tenderloin with the mixture. Roast the tenderloin until the internal temperature reaches 140°F, 18 to 20 minutes. Let the meat rest for 10 minutes before slicing diagonally.

Serves: 4
Prep Time: 10 minutes
Cooking Time: 25 minutes

LATIN SABOR

- CHILAQUILES
- TJ TORTILLA SOUP
- WHITE GAZPACHO
- ROASTED CORN AND CHILE CHOWDER
- CARNE ASADA SALAD
- ARROZ VERDE
- MEXI-CORN
- SHERRY MUSHROOMS WITH PANCETTA
- CALABACITAS TRADER JOSÉ
- SHRIMP COCKTAIL WITH SALSA VERDE
- TEQUILA SHRIMP
- SPANISH-STYLE PORK
- PEPITA PORK
- GAMBAS Y JAMÓN
- CARNITAS QUESADILLAS
- MARGARITA PORK CHOPS
- CHIMICHURRI SAUCE

Latin flavors are ubiquitous in Southern California, where I live. My small town has fewer than ten restaurants, and three are Mexican! The palate of flavors is vibrant and *picante*, perfect for warm evenings on the patio. Whether the focus is Mexican, Spanish, or South American, you can expect your taste buds to be dancing to a flamenco beat from each bold bite. Trader Joe's carries some terrific ingredients to assemble an array of luscious Latin dishes. From rustic corn and flour tortillas that look handmade, to prepackaged guacamole kits, to a sizeable selection of salsas, not to mention no-cook frozen options, there are plenty of ways to get your spicy flavor fix at Trader José's.

CHILAQUILES

A Mexican mom's clever use of leftover tortillas, chilaquiles is one of my favorite breakfasts. Or lunches. Yes, dinner, too. Who doesn't love breakfast for dinner? This casserole is a great vehicle for leftover cooked chicken or pork. Cube or shred the cooked meat and add it with the sautéed vegetables. If you have leftover Trader Joe's Corn and Chile Tomato-Less Salsa, that is terrific tossed in, too.

1 tablespoon grapeseed oil

1 medium onion, thinly sliced

1 medium red bell pepper, thinly sliced

1 medium zucchini, sliced

¼ teaspoon ground cumin

12 (6-inch) corn tortillas, cut into bite-size pieces

2 cups shredded Jack or cheddar cheese, or a combination

1 (4-ounce) can Trader Joe's New Mexico Hatch Valley Fire-Roasted Diced Green Chiles

4 eggs

2 cups buttermilk

½ teaspoon salt

several grinds black pepper

VEGETARIAN, GLUTEN-FREE (IF GLUTEN-FREE TORTILLAS ARE USED)

Preheat the oven to 375°F. In a medium sauté pan or skillet, heat the grapeseed oil over medium heat. Sauté the onion about 3 minutes. Add the red bell pepper and sauté until just softened, about 2 minutes. Add the zucchini and cumin and continue to sauté until all the vegetables are tender, 3 to 4 minutes. Transfer to a plate and cool to room temperature.

Spread half the tortilla pieces in the bottom of a 9 x 13-inch ovenproof casserole dish. Sprinkle half the cheese and half the chiles over the top. Add the sautéed vegetables and top with the remaining tortilla pieces. Sprinkle the remaining cheese and chiles on top.

In a medium bowl, beat the eggs slightly, just to break them up, then add the buttermilk. Add the salt and pepper, and stir to combine. Pour over the casserole and bake until bubbling and brown, 35 to 40 minutes.

Serves: 4 to 6
Prep Time: 15 minutes
Cooking Time: 1 hour

TJ TORTILLA SOUP

My family rates a Mexican restaurant on the strength of their tortilla soup. This one is the brothy type, as opposed to the masa-thickened kind. I love the kaleidoscope look of the multicolored vegetables and the spicy crunch of the tortilla strips. Go garnish crazy!

1 tablespoon grapeseed oil or canola oil

1 cup chopped onion

1 teaspoon ground cumin

1 tablespoon Trader Joe's Taco Seasoning Mix

6 cups chicken broth

1 (15-ounce) can diced tomatoes in juice

1 (15-ounce) can kidney beans, drained and rinsed

1 (15-ounce) can black beans, drained and rinsed

1 cup shredded carrots

1 (4-ounce) can Trader Joe's New Mexico Hatch Valley Fire Roasted Diced Green Chiles

3 ribs celery, sliced ¼ inch thick

1 (12-ounce) package Trader Joe's Just Grilled Chicken Strips, chopped

salt and freshly ground black pepper

SEASONED TORTILLA STRIPS:

3 tablespoons grapeseed oil or canola oil

4 (6-inch) corn tortillas, cut into ¼-inch strips

Trader Joe's Taco Seasoning Mix

GLUTEN-FREE (IF GLUTEN-FREE TORTILLAS ARE USED)

In a large saucepan, heat the oil over medium-high heat. Sauté the onion until barely tender, about 5 minutes. Add the cumin and taco seasoning, and cook until fragrant, about 2 minutes. Add the chicken broth and tomatoes, and bring to a boil. Lower the heat to medium, add the kidney beans, black beans, carrots, chiles, and celery, and simmer for 10 minutes. Add the chicken and warm through. Adjust the seasoning with salt, pepper, and more taco seasoning, if desired. Keep the soup hot while you make the chips.

For the tortilla strips: While the soup simmers, fry the tortilla strips in batches. Heat the oil in a sauté pan or skillet over high heat, and carefully add about one-quarter of the strips. Turn them with tongs, and cook until golden and crisp, 1 to 2 minutes. Transfer to layers of paper towels, and season with taco seasoning mix while still hot. Garnish each bowl of soup with a generous sprinkle of tortilla strips.

Serves: 4
Prep Time: 10 minutes
Cooking Time: 30 minutes

Set out bowls of chopped cilantro, grated cheese, crème fraîche or sour cream, avocado slices, and extra seasoned tortilla strips, and let your gang customize their soup experience.

WHITE GAZPACHO

A no-less-traditional version of the usual tomato-based gazpacho, this elegant chilled beauty is fun to serve in shot glasses. Just be prepared to refill those little guys, because folks love this stuff.

2 cups chicken or vegetable broth

2 cups stale Trader Joe's Pain Pascal Organic Demi Miche or another hearty bread, torn into bite-size pieces

1 cup slivered blanched almonds

2 cups green grapes

2 Persian cucumbers, ends trimmed, and cut into 4 pieces each

2 cubes frozen crushed garlic

2 tablespoons white balsamic vinegar

¼ cup olive oil

salt

chives or halved red and green grapes, for garnish

VEGAN (IF VEGETABLE BROTH IS USED)

In a medium saucepan over high heat, bring the broth to a boil. Place the bread cubes in a large heatproof bowl, and pour the hot broth over the bread. Let stand until most of the liquid is absorbed, about 15 minutes. Transfer the bread and any remaining liquid to a food processor and pulse to chop. Add the almonds, grapes, cucumbers, and garlic. Pulse to puree. Add the vinegar and pulse to combine. With the motor running, stream in the olive oil through the feed tube until incorporated. Chill. Season to taste with salt and additional vinegar. Garnish with chives or grapes.

Serves: 4 to 6
Prep Time: 10 minutes
Cooking Time: 5 minutes

CALABACITAS TRADER JOSÉ

One of my very favorite vegetable dishes, these "little squashes" are gorgeous and good for you. Also, they're amazingly tasty. Grab your keys and head to TJ's—you want this now. Trader Joe's Shredded Pepper Jack Cheese Blend or Fancy Shredded Mexican Blend is a great choice for the cheese. Try this delicious vegetable sauté folded into a tortilla.

2 tablespoons olive oil

1 medium red onion, sliced

2 cubes frozen crushed garlic

2 medium zucchini, sliced

2 medium yellow squash, sliced

1 (16-ounce) bag frozen roasted corn

1 (4-ounce) can Trader Joe's New Mexico Hatch Valley Fire-Roasted Diced Green Chiles

handful of Trader Joe's Mixed Medley Cherry Tomatoes or Mini Heirloom Tomatoes

1½ cups shredded cheese, divided

salt and freshly ground black pepper

VEGETARIAN, GLUTEN-FREE

In a large sauté pan or skillet, heat the olive oil over medium-high heat. Sauté the onion until softened, about 4 minutes. Add the garlic and sauté until fragrant, 1 to 2 minutes. Add the zucchini and yellow squash, and sauté until softened, 3 to 4 minutes. Add the corn and sauté until warmed through, 3 to 4 minutes. Add the chiles and tomatoes and sauté until warmed through, 2 to 3 minutes. Add 1 cup cheese, and season to taste with salt and pepper. Stir to combine, place in a serving dish, and top with the remaining cheese.

Serves: 4
Prep Time: 10 minutes
Cooking Time: 15 minutes

SHRIMP COCKTAIL *with* SALSA VERDE

Quick, summery, and so, so tasty. Instead of the traditional martini glass, a margarita glass would make for a great presentation.

1 pound cooked shrimp, thawed if frozen

1 ripe avocado, cubed

½ red onion, finely chopped

½ cup Trader Joe's Corn and Chile Tomato-Less Salsa

½ cup Trader Joe's Salsa Verde

juice of 1 lime

salt and freshly ground black pepper

GLUTEN-FREE

Combine the shrimp, avocado, onion, corn salsa, salsa verde, and lime juice in a large bowl. Season to taste with salt and pepper, and add more lime juice or more salsa verde, if desired.

Serves: 4
Prep Time: 5 minutes
Cooking Time: none

TEQUILA SHRIMP

If shrimp isn't your thing, substitute chunks of chicken—it will still have great margarita flavor and vibrant veggie colors.

1 tablespoon grapeseed oil

1 medium yellow onion, chopped

3 cubes frozen crushed garlic

1 pound uncooked large shrimp, peeled and deveined

¼ cup tequila

2 medium ripe tomatoes, chopped

½ cup shredded carrots

juice of 2 limes

1 ripe avocado, cubed

salt and freshly ground black pepper

In a medium sauté pan or skillet, heat the grapeseed oil over medium-high heat. Sauté the onion until it begins to soften, 3 to 4 minutes. Add the garlic and sauté until fragrant, 1 to 2 minutes. Add the shrimp and sauté until just pink, 3 to 4 minutes. Remove from the heat and carefully add the tequila. (Or leave it on the heat and flambé if you want some drama, but have a lid nearby to quell the flame, if necessary). Return the pan to the heat, add the tomatoes and carrots, and sauté for 2 minutes. Add the lime juice and cook until the shrimp is just pink and opaque, about 1 minute more. Add the avocado, and toss to warm through. Season to taste with salt and pepper.

Serves: 4 as an appetizer, 2 to 3 as a main course

Prep Time: 10 minutes

Cooking Time: 15 minutes

SPANISH-STYLE PORK

Traditional Spanish tapas ingredients make this dish sing. I serve it as a main dish, or as part of a tapas party.

1 (¾ to 1-pound) pork tenderloin, cut into ½-inch-thick medallions (rounds)

salt and freshly ground black pepper

2 tablespoons olive oil, divided

2 cubes frozen crushed garlic

2 cups sliced white or crimini mushrooms

½ cup dry sherry

¾ cup orange juice, divided

½ cup sliced Trader Joe's Manzanilla Olives with Pimientos (optional)

GLUTEN-FREE

Season the pork with salt and pepper. Heat 1 tablespoon olive oil in a medium sauté pan or skillet over medium-high heat. Brown the pork on both sides and set aside. Add the remaining 1 tablespoon olive oil, and sauté the garlic until fragrant, 2 to 3 minutes. Add the mushrooms, and sauté until the released moisture evaporates, about 5 minutes. Transfer to a platter. Combine the sherry with ½ cup orange juice, and pour into the sauté pan or skillet. Bring to a boil, lower the heat to medium, and simmer for about 3 minutes. Return the pork to the pan, and simmer until cooked through, 2 to 4 minutes. Transfer the pork to a serving platter. Add the remaining ¼ cup orange juice to the pan, and simmer until the sauce thickens slightly, about 2 minutes. Stir the olives into the mushrooms, and scrape the mixture onto the pork. Pour the sauce on top and serve.

Serves: 4
Prep Time: 10 minutes
Cooking Time: 20 minutes

PEPITA PORK

You'll love the flavors of this dish. The nuttiness of the pumpkinseeds brings a great depth of flavor, and the jalapeño and cilantro brighten everything they touch. If you're lucky enough to have leftovers, they make a great filling for quesadillas or the yummy Mexican sandwiches served on a burger bun called cemitas.

1 (1½-pound) pork tenderloin, cut into ½-inch-thick medallions (rounds)

salt and freshly ground black pepper

1 tablespoon olive oil

1½ cups pepitas (pumpkinseeds)

1 jalapeño chile, seeded and cut into strips

½ medium onion, chopped

2 cubes frozen crushed garlic

1 cup fresh cilantro leaves

½ teaspoon ground cumin

1 to 1½ cups chicken broth

½ cup cream

Season the pork with salt and pepper. In a medium sauté pan or skillet, heat the olive oil over high heat. Working in batches, brown the pork on both sides. Transfer the pork to a warm platter. In a small sauté pan or skillet, toast the pepitas until aromatic, 2 to 3 minutes. In a food processor, coarsely chop the pepitas. Add the jalapeño, onion, garlic, cilantro, and cumin and coarsely chop. With the motor running, stream in enough chicken broth to puree the mixture to the consistency of heavy cream. In the sauté pan or skillet used to brown the pork, cook the pepita mixture until thickened and aromatic, about 5 minutes. Add the cream and warm through. Add the pork and any accumulated juices to the pepita sauce. Simmer until the pork is barely pink in the center, about 5 minutes. Adjust the seasoning with salt and pepper.

Serves: 4 to 6
Prep Time: 10 minutes
Cooking Time: 20 minutes

GAMBAS Y JAMÓN

Here's another classic tapa that can be served as a main dish. I love the combination of garlicky shrimp, savory pork, and a little spice. Serve it on toasts—"montaditos" en español—for a great Spanish appetizer.

1 tablespoon olive oil

1 tablespoon butter

1 pound uncooked large shrimp, peeled and deveined (reserve the shells, if you peel them)

5 cubes frozen crushed garlic

¼ cup chopped Serrano ham, pancetta, or prosciutto

salt and freshly ground black pepper

Trader Joe's Chili Pepper Hot Sauce or Jalapeño Pepper Hot Sauce

GLUTEN-FREE

In a sauté pan or skillet large enough to hold the shrimp in a single layer, heat the olive oil and butter to bubbling over medium-high heat. If you have the shrimp shells, sauté until they turn pink and the oil-butter mixture is perfumed with the aroma of shrimp. Remove the shells with tongs or a slotted spoon, shaking the liquid back into the pan. Add the garlic and sauté until fragrant, 2 to 3 minutes. Add the ham, and sauté for 2 minutes. Add the shrimp and sauté just until just pink and opaque, 2 to 4 minutes. Season to taste with salt, pepper, and hot sauce. Serve on baguette toasts as an appetizer or over rice for a main dish.

Serves: 4 as an appetizer, 2 to 3 as a main course
Prep Time: 10 minutes
Cooking Time: 15 minutes

CARNITAS QUESADILLAS

Carnitas take hours and hours to simmer to pull-apart tender perfection, but Joe did the work for us on this one. Don't be put off by the hard plastic brick package—a quick microwaving brings the meat to perfect melting texture. I love the Trader Joe's Shredded Pepper Jack Cheese Blend or Fancy Shredded Mexican Blend in this dish.

1 (16-ounce) package Trader Joe's Handmade Corn Tortillas (you'll need 8)

1 (12-ounce) bottle Trader Joe's Cilantro Salad Dressing Reduced Fat (in the refrigerated section)

1 (12-ounce) package Trader José's Traditional Carnitas, shredded

1 cup shredded cheese blend

1 tablespoon grapeseed oil or canola oil

GARNISHES:

salsa

guacamole

sliced limes

Start with two tortillas. Spread about 2 teaspoons cilantro dressing on one side of each tortilla. Shred about 3 tablespoons carnitas and scatter on top of one of the tortillas. Scatter about ¼ cup cheese on top of the carnitas. Top with the second tortilla, plain side up. Repeat with the remaining ingredients until you have assembled four quesadillas. Heat the oil in a medium sauté pan or skillet over medium heat. Carefully place one quesadilla into the oil. Cook until the bottom side is golden and just crispy, about 4 minutes. With a spatula, carefully flip the quesadilla and cook until the second side is golden and crisp, about 3 minutes. Transfer to a paper towel and let cool slightly before cutting into quarters. Repeat with the remaining quesadillas. Serve with salsa, guacamole, and sliced limes, if using.

Serves: 4
Prep Time: 15 minutes
Cooking Time: 15 minutes

MARGARITA PORK CHOPS

One of the best features of this recipe is that it includes nearly everything necessary to stir up a batch of margaritas! So perhaps that should be Step 1 in the instructions?

1 teaspoon ground cumin

2 teaspoons salt

½ teaspoon freshly ground black pepper

4 Trader Joe's Butcher Shop Bone-In Frenched Center-Cut Pork Chops

¼ cup chicken broth

½ cup tequila

2 tablespoons fresh lime juice

1 tablespoon olive oil

3 cubes frozen crushed garlic

4 tablespoons butter

½ jalapeño chile, seeded and minced

Combine the cumin, salt, and pepper in a small bowl. Season the pork chops well on both sides with this mixture. (You may have some seasoning mix left over.) In another bowl, combine the chicken broth, tequila, and lime juice. In a large sauté pan or skillet, heat the olive oil over medium-high heat. Brown the chops well, 4 to 5 minutes per side. Transfer the chops to a warm platter. In the same pan, sauté the garlic until fragrant, 1 to 2 minutes. Remove the pan from the heat, add the broth mixture, and return to the heat. (Have a lid ready to cover the pan in case the alcohol ignites; by combining the liquids, the alcohol has been diluted, but it may flare up.) Bring the mixture to a boil and reduce to about ¼ cup. Add the butter and any juices that have accumulated on the platter. Swirl the pan until the butter is incorporated. Season to taste with the jalapeño, salt, and pepper. Pour the sauce over the chops.

Serves: 4
Prep Time: 10 minutes
Cooking Time: 20 minutes

CHIMICHURRI SAUCE

Trader Joe's used to carry chimichurri *sauce, and it's one of their discontinued items whose absence I mourn most. Luckily, it's not too much trouble to re-create. Originating in Argentina, where they love their beef, this herby, vibrant shot of green goodness is great on steak, but also on poultry, over grilled vegetables, or tossed with rice.*

1 (.75-ounce) package fresh organic Italian parsley

2 tablespoons chopped fresh cilantro or oregano (optional)

3 cubes frozen crushed garlic

½ cup olive oil

2 tablespoons red wine vinegar or fresh lemon juice

salt and freshly ground black pepper

red chile pepper flakes

VEGAN (IF USED ON RICE, VEGETABLES), GLUTEN-FREE

Place the parsley and other herbs, if using, in a mortar and pestle or food processor, and grind or pulse to coarsely chop. Add the garlic and grind or pulse to chop. Add the olive oil and vinegar or lemon juice and combine well. Season to taste with salt, pepper, and chile pepper flakes.

Makes: about ½ cup

Prep Time: 5 minutes

Cooking Time: none

There are many variations to a basic *chimichurri*. Add grated onion, if you like, or use lime juice in place of the vinegar. Try more garlic, if you dare . . .

ALL-AMERICAN

- FARM SKILLET FRITTATA
- BREAKFAST TACO BAR
- CHILE AND CRAB CHOWDER
- ROADHOUSE STEAK AND BEER CHILI
- CORN PUDDIN'
- ROASTED BUTTERNUT SQUASH WITH PECANS, DRIED CHERRIES, AND BLUE CHEESE
- MAQUE CHOUX CAKES
- PULLED PORK SANDWICHES
- CRISPY BAKED CHICKEN
- PORK CHOPS ÉTOUFÉE
- SLOPPY T-JOE'S
- BOURBON BBQ RIBS
- MAC DADDY MAC 'N' CHEESE
- LEMON-LOADED MERINGUE-TOPPED CUPCAKES
- HOT TIN ROOF SUNDAE

Trader Joe's was founded in the good old USA. While it may be German owned and feature ingredients from all over the world, it's American at its core. Stanford-educated visionary Joe Coulombe created the South Seas island–themed chain to cater to overeducated, underemployed folks with a taste for the good life. He targeted those "Europe on $5 a day" backpackers and brought them the pleasurable stuff they had discovered on their travels, at prices they could still manage after buying the plane ticket home. And, boy, did it work! The stores have spread to both coasts and are oozing toward the middle, bringing great wines (state law permitting), low-priced cheese, and other snackables to the masses. A tip of the hat to my American hero, *the* Trader Joe!

FARM SKILLET FRITTATA

This goes together really quickly, and is so satisfying. I'd eat it for breakfast, lunch, or dinner!

½ pound sausage, uncooked and crumbled, or precooked and cubed

1 tablespoon butter or canola oil

1 (16-ounce) bag frozen Trader Joe's Country Potatoes with Haricots Verts and Wild Mushrooms

4 eggs

salt and freshly ground black pepper

2 ounces crumbled goat or feta cheese, or Trader Joe's Shredded Smoked Cheese Blend (optional)

GLUTEN-FREE

If using uncooked sausage, in a medium nonstick sauté pan or skillet over medium heat, cook the crumbled sausage until no longer pink, about 5 minutes. If using precooked sausages, heat the butter or canola oil in the sauté pan or skillet and cook the sausage cubes until browned, about 5 minutes. Remove the sausage, leaving about 1 tablespoon of the sausage drippings in the pan. Add the vegetables and sauté until thawed, about 6 minutes. In a medium bowl, whisk the eggs to combine. Pour into the pan with the vegetables. Add the sausage to the pan, stirring gently to combine. Season with salt and pepper. Cover the pan, reduce the heat to low, and cook until the eggs are just set, about 4 minutes. Add the cheese, if using, cover the pan again, and cook until the cheese softens. Cut the frittata into wedges to serve.

Serves: 4 to 6
Prep Time: 5 minutes
Cooking Time: 20 minutes

BREAKFAST TACO BAR

It took a trip to Austin, Texas, to introduce me to the concept of breakfast tacos. Where have they been all my life? Food trucks all over town make them—I even grabbed one at the airport. There are many filling options, and even more delicious combinations. They make a great alternative to muffins at a morning meeting.

FILLING SUGGESTIONS:

scrambled eggs

sautéed onions and peppers

roasted potatoes

grated cheese

cooked bacon

cooked Soyrizo

corn or flour tortillas

sliced avocados

salsa

VEGAN, GLUTEN-FREE (DEPENDING ON TORTILLAS AND FILLINGS USED)

Assemble filling ingredients as desired. To warm tortillas, quickly toast them over the flame of a gas burner, turning with tongs after about 15 seconds. You can also heat them in a microwave or wrapped in foil in a 375°F oven for about 20 minutes, or heat them on a griddle or comal griddle. Then just grab a tortilla, add your fillings of choice, and dig in.

Serves: varies
Prep Time: depends on fillings
Cooking Time: varies

CHILE *and* CRAB CHOWDER

Chowders can be creamy or chunky, red or white, simple or fancy. This one is just terrific and takes only a half hour to simmer to creamy perfection. Use the remaining crab for crab cakes, or toss into hot pasta. A boiling potato (labeled at TJ's as Baby Red Potatoes, Baby Dutch Yellow Potatoes, or Potato Medley—Red, Gold, and Purple) has a thinner, smoother skin than a russet, or baking, potato. When simmered, these babies will hold their shape better than a russet, which tends to fall apart.

2 tablespoons butter

1 medium onion, chopped

4 cups vegetable or chicken broth

1 medium boiling potato, cubed

1 teaspoon chopped fresh thyme

1 (4-ounce) can Trader Joe's New Mexico Hatch Valley Fire-Roasted Diced Green Chiles

1 cup corn kernels, fresh or frozen

½ pound refrigerated canned crabmeat

½ cup half-and-half or heavy cream

½ cup grated sharp cheddar cheese

dash of Trader Joe's Chili Pepper Hot Sauce or Jalapeño Pepper Hot Sauce

salt and freshly ground black pepper

GLUTEN-FREE

Heat the butter in a saucepan over medium-high heat. Sauté the onion until it begins to soften, about 5 minutes. Add the broth, potato, and thyme, and bring to a boil. Reduce the heat to low and simmer until the potatoes are tender, about 15 minutes. Stir in the chiles and corn. Add the crabmeat and the half-and-half or cream and warm through. Remove from the heat, stir in the cheddar, and allow the heat of the chowder to melt the cheese. Season to taste with hot sauce, salt, and pepper.

Serves: 4 to 6
Prep Time: 5 minutes
Cooking Time: less than 30 minutes

ROADHOUSE STEAK *and* BEER CHILI

Double meat and a dose of beer make for a hearty bowl of goodness.
You'll need only half the bottle of beer for the recipe, but I think you'll
figure out some way to deal with the other half while you cook . . .

2 tablespoons olive oil or
grapeseed oil

½ pound ground beef

1½ pounds Trader Joe's Very
Thinly Sliced Sirloin

1 medium onion, chopped

4 cubes frozen crushed garlic

1 (1-pint) package Trader Joe's
Minisweet Peppers, chopped

1 (1.3-ounce) package Trader
Joe's Taco Seasoning

1 (15-ounce) can kidney beans,
drained and rinsed (optional)

1 (15-ounce) can Organic Diced
Fire-Roasted Tomatoes with
Organic Green Chiles

2 teaspoons ground cumin

½ (12-ounce) bottle Fat Weasel
Ale, or other beer

salt and freshly ground black
pepper

In a medium saucepan, heat the oil over medium-high heat. Sauté the ground beef until no longer pink, about 5 minutes. Add the sirloin and sauté until no longer pink, 3 to 4 minutes. Add the onion and sauté until softened, 3 to 4 minutes. Add the garlic and sauté until fragrant, 2 to 3 minutes. Add the peppers and sauté until softened, 3 to 4 minutes. Add the taco seasoning and sauté until fragrant, 2 to 3 minutes. Add the beans, if using, and the tomatoes, cumin, and beer. Bring to a boil, then reduce the heat to low and simmer until the meat is cooked and the sauce has reduced, 35 to 40 minutes. Season to taste with salt and pepper.

Serves: 4 to 6
Prep Time: 10 minutes
Cooking Time: 1 hour

CORN PUDDIN'

A summertime staple in the South, corn pudding makes a great side dish for barbecued ribs or chicken. I used to make it to mark the loss of my kids' front teeth—so hard to eat corn on the cob when you miss half the kernels! A little grated Parmesan or cheddar over the top of this wouldn't hurt anything, would it?

2 tablespoons butter or bacon fat, plus more for preparing the dish

1 medium red bell pepper, chopped

½ cup chopped red onion

kernels from 5 ears corn, or 4 cups frozen corn kernels

4 eggs

2 cups half-and-half or milk

salt and freshly ground black pepper

3 strips bacon, cooked until crisp and chopped (optional)

Preheat the oven to 350°F. In a medium sauté pan or skillet over medium-high heat, melt the butter or bacon fat. Sauté the bell pepper and onion until softened, about 4 minutes. Add the corn and sauté until just warmed through, 1 to 2 minutes for fresh corn, 3 to 5 minutes for frozen. Set aside. In a large bowl, whisk the eggs to combine. Whisk in the half-and-half or milk, and season lightly with salt and pepper. Stir in the corn mixture and bacon, if using. Butter an 8 x 8-inch casserole dish and pour in the batter. Bake until puffed and golden, about 30 minutes.

Serves: 4
Prep Time: 10 minutes
Cooking Time: 40 minutes

ROASTED BUTTERNUT SQUASH with PECANS, DRIED CHERRIES, and BLUE CHEESE

Can you please make this immediately? It is just about the prettiest thing you can put on a platter, and it's just so delish. It's one of my favorite sides in autumn—try it on top of salad greens, too.

1½ (12-ounce) bags Trader Joe's Cut Butternut Squash

1 medium red onion, sliced

salt and freshly ground black pepper

pinch of dried sage

1 tablespoon olive oil, more or less

½ cup chopped pecans

¼ cup dried cherries

¼ cup crumbled Maytag or other blue cheese

VEGETARIAN

Preheat the oven to 400°F. Arrange the squash and onion in a single layer on a rimmed baking sheet. Season with salt, pepper, and sage, and drizzle with olive oil. Roast until barely tender, 15 to 20 minutes. Scatter the pecans over the top and roast until the vegetables are tender, about 5 minutes longer. Remove the squash mixture from the oven, and toss with the dried cherries and blue cheese. Adjust the seasoning with salt and pepper.

Serves: 4
Prep Time: 5 minutes
Cooking Time: 20 minutes

MAQUE CHOUX CAKES

Perfect party fare, these are great with or without the shrimp. They disappear fast from party platters, so double or triple the batch if you're feeding a crowd. These are one of the few foods I've encountered that are as good—or better—baked as they are fried. Hooray! Baking powder is seasonal at TJ's, so grab it when you spot it.

1 egg

4 tablespoons milk

½ cup flour

pinch of baking powder

½ cup finely chopped uncooked shrimp

1½ cups Trader Joe's Corn and Chile Tomato-Less Salsa

pinch of salt

Preheat the oven to 425°F and lightly oil a rimmed baking sheet. In a medium bowl, whisk together the egg and milk. Add the flour and baking powder and stir to combine. The mixture will be thick. Stir in the chopped shrimp, salsa, and salt. Spoon dollops of the mixture onto the prepared pan, leaving 1½ inches between the cakes. Bake for 10 minutes, flip with a spatula, and bake until golden, 10 minutes longer. Serve immediately.

Serves: 4
Prep Time: 5 minutes
Cooking Time: 20 minutes

PULLED PORK SANDWICHES

A pulled pork sandwich is heaven on a plate as far as I'm concerned: sweet-tangy sauce, crunchy coleslaw, and pork goodness. These go together so quickly, because Joe did almost all the work!

1 (16-ounce) package Trader Joe's Pulled Pork in Smoky BBQ Sauce

½ (10-ounce) bag shredded cabbage

handful of shredded carrots

½ cup organic mayonnaise

2 tablespoons red wine vinegar

salt and freshly ground black pepper

4 Trader Joe's Panini Rustic Rolls

Heat the pork according to the package directions. While the pork is heating, in a large bowl, combine the cabbage and carrots. In a small bowl, stir together the mayonnaise and vinegar. Toss the cabbage and carrots with the dressing. Season to taste with salt and pepper. Split the rolls horizontally and toast. Divide the pork among the rolls, and serve the slaw in the sandwiches or on the side.

Serves: 4
Prep Time: 10 minutes
Cooking Time: 5 minutes

CRISPY BAKED CHICKEN

Some versions of this recipe call it "oven-fried chicken." Now, to me, fried is fried, and this ain't that. Fried chicken is some people's idea of heaven, but it's a pain to make. This version is crisp and tasty, without the spattering oil and mess. You can still lick your fingers, though.

3 pounds Trader Joe's All-Natural Split Breasts, Thighs, and Drumsticks, or other bone-in chicken pieces

1 quart buttermilk

1 (12-ounce) box Trader Joe's Organic Corn Flakes

salt and freshly ground black pepper

cayenne pepper

Place the chicken in a casserole dish or two sealable plastic bags. Cover the chicken with the buttermilk, and refrigerate to marinate for at least 2 hours or overnight.

Preheat the oven to 400°F. In a large bowl, crush the corn flakes into crumbs. Season with salt, black pepper, and a pinch or more of cayenne. One at a time, remove the chicken pieces from the buttermilk and coat with the seasoned corn flake crumbs. Place on a rimmed baking sheet. Repeat until all the chicken is coated, then discard the marinade. Roast until the chicken's internal temperature reaches 155°F, 35 to 40 minutes.

Serves: 4
Prep Time: 10 minutes, plus marinating time
Cooking Time: 40 minutes

PORK CHOPS ÉTOUFÉE

I count New Orleans among my favorite spots on the planet. In the Crescent City, étoufée *means smothered, and I'd happily be smothered with these tender tasty chops. Traditionally,* étoufées *are served atop long-grain white rice, but brown rice works, too. Buttered noodles are also great.*

6 pork chops, each ¾ to 1 inch thick

salt and freshly ground black pepper

2 teaspoons olive oil

2 tablespoons butter

1 medium onion, chopped

3 cubes frozen crushed garlic

1 cup chopped Trader Joe's Minisweet Peppers

½ cup finely chopped celery

2 tablespoons flour

1 (14.5-ounce) can Trader Joe's Organic Diced and Fire-Roasted Tomatoes with Organic Green Chiles

2 cups chicken broth

Trader Joe's Chili Pepper Hot Sauce or Jalapeño Pepper Hot Sauce

GLUTEN-FREE

Lightly season the pork chops with salt and pepper. In a large sauté pan or skillet, heat the olive oil over medium-high heat. Brown the pork chops, about 3 minutes on each side. Transfer to a plate and set aside. In the same pan, melt the butter over high heat. Sauté the onion until softened and fragrant, about 4 minutes. Add the garlic and sauté until fragrant, 1 to 2 minutes. Add the peppers and celery, and sauté until softened, 3 to 4 minutes. Add the flour, stir to coat the vegetables, and cook for 4 minutes. Add the tomatoes and chicken broth, stir, and bring to a boil. Reduce the heat to low and add the pork chops to the sauce. Cover and simmer until the pork chops are cooked through and the flour loses its raw aroma, 20 to 25 minutes. Add 1 teaspoon hot sauce or to taste. Stir and adjust the seasoning with salt and pepper.

Serves: 4 to 6

Prep Time: 10 minutes

Cooking Time: 40 minutes

I prefer bone-in pork chops, but boneless loin chops also work well. If pork chops aren't your thing, you can "smother" some chicken pieces instead.

SLOPPY T-JOE'S

This is great on one of those carpool-practice-snack-homework kinda nights. These Joe's also freeze well, so make a double batch for the next time the family schedule gets hectic.

2 tablespoons olive oil

2 medium onions, chopped

6 cubes frozen crushed garlic

1 jalapeño chile, chopped

1 medium green bell pepper, chopped

4 ribs celery, chopped

2 pounds ground beef or ground turkey

1 (15-ounce) can tomato sauce

2 tablespoons tomato paste

½ cup Trader Joe's Bold and Smoky Kansas City-Style Barbecue Sauce

Trader Joe's Chili Pepper Hot Sauce or Jalapeño Pepper Hot Sauce

6 hamburger buns

In a medium sauté pan or skillet, heat the olive oil over high heat. Sauté the onions until softened, 4 to 5 minutes. Add the garlic and jalapeño, and sauté until fragrant, about 2 minutes. Add the bell pepper and celery, and sauté for 3 minutes longer. Add the ground meat and sauté until no longer pink, 5 to 6 minutes. Add the tomato sauce, tomato paste, and barbecue sauce.

Add 1 teaspoon of the hot sauce or to taste. Simmer until the sauce is thickened, about 10 minutes. While the filling is thickening, toast the buns. Serve on the buns.

Serves: 6
Prep Time: 10 minutes
Cooking Time: 30 minutes

BOURBON BBQ RIBS

Gotta love Alton Brown, the Food Network's resident food science geek. These ribs are a riff on a technique I saw him do years ago, and it's been my go-to way to cook ribs ever since. Alton uses the flavorful braising liquid as a glaze for the ribs, but I like some barbecue sauce on there, too.

¼ cup brown sugar

1 tablespoon Trader Joe's 21 Seasoning Salute

1 tablespoon salt

2 cubes frozen crushed garlic

1 (2 to 2½-pound) rack pork baby back ribs (12 to 15 ribs)

½ cup water

3 tablespoons bourbon, divided

1 cup Trader Joe's All-Natural Barbecue Sauce

2 tablespoons Trader Joe's Hot and Sweet Mustard

Preheat the oven to 300°F. Line a rimmed baking sheet with a long swath of foil, about 30 inches, with the ends overhanging the long (17-inch) sides of the pan. In a small bowl, combine the brown sugar, seasoning mix, salt, and garlic. Rub on both sides of the ribs, and set them in the foil, curved side up. Pull the edges of the foil up to partially enclose the ribs. Combine the water with 1 tablespoon bourbon and pour into the foil packet. Crimp the long edges of the foil together to enclose the ribs completely. Bake 2 hours. In a small bowl, combine the barbecue sauce with the remaining 2 tablespoons bourbon and the mustard. Remove the ribs from the pan, pour off the liquid, then return the ribs to the pan. Increase the oven temperature to 400°F. Generously brush the ribs with the sauce and return to the oven, cooking until the ribs are glazed, about 8 minutes. Cut into sections to serve.

Serves: 4 to 6

Prep Time: 10 minutes

Cooking Time: 2 hours 15 minutes

Oh, Joe, you make me laugh sometimes. After several years' absence, my beloved Hot and Sweet Mustard reappeared on the shelves, but I was devastated when it disappeared again. I was told it's now stocked seasonally—for "ham season." What season is *that*, I wonder? By my calculations, it seems to be November to April (Thanksgiving through Easter), so hoard accordingly.

JULIENNE—This technique produces those thin strips or sticks you see in the restaurants without a lot of work. By cutting thick strips of vegetables or meat and then stacking a few of those strips and gliding your chef's knife through them again (the long way), you'll get thinner strips. Need even thinner ones? Just stack and glide again. (Kinda the "lather, rinse, repeat" of the kitchen!) Until your knife skills are rocking, don't make the stacks too high. Better to be safe than get stitches.

SAUTÉ—Technically, this means to make the food *jump* in the pan, with that impressive arc, like TV chefs do. In our Chez Cherie Basic Cooking series, we encourage students to practice this with a snack-size resealable plastic bag half-full of M&Ms. Once they've mastered the flip (in a room-temperature pan, of course—a hot pan would make this whole thing impossible!), they get to try it with loose candies. Muuuch harder, but I tell them they can eat the ones that jump out! If you want to skip this exercise, you can just use tongs or a spatula to get the food moving in the pan. The main idea is for the food to cook on all sides, so whether flipping, nudging, or turning it over with a spatula, the end result will be the same. I usually prefer a regular pan, not a nonstick pan, for sautéing because the untreated surface seems to heat faster and more evenly, allowing that lovely film of flavor to develop on the bottom of the pan.

HOARDABLES AND PANTRY STAPLES

We all know that TJ's shelves are full of great stuff, but some items tend to disappear faster than a teenager when the dishwasher needs loading! This is a list of my current must-haves. Some items are seasonal, so I'll stockpile a year's worth of those when I can. (Organic canned pumpkin saved my reputation last year when I fielded a call from a frantic student whose family was counting on a big pot of pumpkin–black bean soup from *The I Love Trader Joe's Cookbook*. I met her at the cooking school with two cans in hand, saving her day and endearing myself to her forever!) Some items are perishable, so I just keep one container in the fridge, while others are shelf-stable, so I like to have four or five jars of those in my pantry at all times. You never know when the supply might be interrupted or a shortage might occur. There is a great sense of comfort to be derived from a well-stocked pantry and a full fridge, and you can create brilliant dishes on the fly if you have some of these hoardables on hand. Take a spin around your kitchen and see what you can come up with from the pantry and refrigerator shelves. Not only that, but if one of your favorite things disappears from the TJ's shelf completely, at least you'll have some of it in reserve so you can wean yourself off it slowly. (I still have one jar of my beloved vanilla paste in my cupboard, but I'm reluctant to use it all up!) You've probably got a hoardables list of your own, but if not, here's mine to get you started.

ACE'S PEAR CIDER

BALSAMIC VINEGAR

BLACK BELUGA LENTILS *(vacuum packaged)*

BLACKTHORN FERMENTED CIDER

BROWNIE TRUFFLE BAKING MIX

BUTTERMILK BISCUITS *(refrigerated)*

CALIFORNIA ESTATE OLIVE OIL

CAPERS IN VINEGAR *(in a jar)*

CARNITAS *(refrigerated)*

CHERRIES, DRIED

CHERRY PRESERVES

CHICKEN SAVORY BROTH CONCENTRATE

COCONUT MILK *(canned)*

CORN AND CHILE TOMATO-LESS SALSA

CORNICHONS

CRABMEAT *(canned, refrigerated)*

CRANBERRIES, FRESH *(seasonal, in produce aisle—freeze in the bag for use all year)*

CRÈME FRAÎCHE

CROISSANTS *(frozen)*

DIJON MUSTARD

EDAMAME, SHELLED *(refrigerated)*

EGGPLANT CAPONATA *(in a jar)*

FARFALLE PASTA

FLEUR DE SEL CARAMEL SAUCE

FROZEN GARLIC CUBES

GENERAL TSAO STIR-FRY SAUCE

GOAT CHEESE *(Trader Joe's Chèvre, Madame Chèvre, or Silver Goat Chèvre)*

GOURMET CHICKEN MEATBALLS WITH SUN-DRIED TOMOATOES, BASIL, AND PROVOLONE

GRAPESEED OIL

GREEK-STYLE FAGE TOTAL YOGURT

GREEN OLIVE TAPENADE

HARVEST GRAINS BLEND

HEAVY CREAM

HOT AND SWEET MUSTARD *(seasonal)*

INDIAN FARE DAL MAKHANI

ISRAELI COUSCOUS

JUST ALMOND MEAL

LEMON CURD *(in a jar)*

MÂCHE LETTUCE

MANGO-GINGER CHUTNEY

MAPLE SYRUP *(Grade B)*

MARCONA ALMONDS

MASCARPONE

MEDJOOL DATES

MINI BURGER BUNS

MINI MILK CHOCOLATE PEANUT BUTTER CUPS

MULTIGRAIN BAKING AND PANCAKE MIX

NEW MEXICO HATCH VALLEY FIRE-ROASTED DICED GREEN CHILES

ORANGE MUSCAT CHAMPAGNE VINEGAR

ORGANIC POLENTA

ORGANIC PUMPKIN PURÉE *(canned, seasonal—holiday)*

ORGANIC QUINOA

PANCETTA, CUBED

PANKO BREAD CRUMBS

PEPITAS *(roasted pumpkin seeds)*

PIZZA DOUGH *(refrigerated)*

POMEGRANATE ARILS *(seasonal)*

POUND PLUS CHOCOLATE BARS

PROSCIUTTO

PUFF PASTRY *(frozen, seasonal)*

PULLED PORK IN SMOKY BBQ SAUCE

PUMPKIN BREAD AND MUFFIN MIX *(seasonal—holiday)*

PUMPKIN BUTTER *(seasonal—holiday)*

RATATOUILLE *(in a jar)*

RED CHILE PEPPER FLAKES

RED WINE VINEGAR

RICE VINEGAR

RICES: BASMATI, JASMINE, ARBORIO, WILD

ROASTED CORN *(frozen)*

ROSEMARY PECANS AND CRANBERRIES

SATAY PEANUT SAUCE

SHALLOTS

SMOKED TROUT IN OLIVE OIL *(canned)*

SOFT LADY FINGERS *(seasonal—holiday)*

SPANISH SAFFRON

SPARKLING LEMONADE

SPICY BROWN MUSTARD

SPICY CHAI LATTE MIX

SPICY, SMOKY PEACH SALSA *(in a jar)*

SWEET CHILI SAUCE

TACO SEASONING MIX

TEENY TINY POTATOES

TRADER GIOTTO'S GENOVA PESTO *(refrigerated)*

TRADER GIOTTO'S ORGANIC VODKA PASTA SAUCE

TRADER JOE'S GOURMET PIE CRUST *(frozen, seasonal—holiday)*

TRIPLE GINGER SNAPS

TURBINADO SUGAR

VANILLA CAKE AND BAKING MIX

VERMOUTH, DRY

WASABI MAYONNAISE

WHOLE WHEAT COUSCOUS

CONVERSIONS

MEASURE	EQUIVALENT	METRIC
1 teaspoon	--	5.0 milliliters
1 tablespoon	3 teaspoons	14.8 milliliters
1 cup	16 tablespoons	236.8 milliliters
1 pint	2 cups	473.6 milliliters
1 quart	4 cups	947.2 milliliters
1 liter	4 cups + 3½ tablespoons	1000 milliliters
1 ounce (dry)	2 tablespoons	28.35 grams
1 pound	16 ounces	453.49 grams
2.21 pounds	35.3 ounces	1 kilogram
325°F/350°F/375°F	--	165°C/177°C/190°C

PHOTO CREDITS

Photos on pages 16, 23, 27, 32, 39, 48, 53, 62, 69, 75, 80, 88, 97, 107, 112, 118, 123, 128, 136, 145, 152, 158, 165, 175, 182 © Judi Swinks Photography. Other photos are credited below:

RECIPE INDEX

INDEX

Most major ingredients are indexed below.

Mushrooms: Bavarian-Style Mushrooms, 65; Champagne Chicken with Champignons, 19; Coquette au Vin, 21; Portobella-Hummus Burgers, 52; Sherry Mushrooms with Pancetta, 156; Spanish-Style Pork, 161; Warm Mushroom Salad, 63

Naan: Potato and Cauliflower Bhaji, 106
Nectarines: Fruit Bathed in Watermelon, 58
Noodles, rice: Fast Faux Pho, 116
Nuts. *See specific nuts* (Pecans; Walnuts; *etc.*)

Okra: Peanut Soup, 74
Olives: Horiatiki Salata (Greek Village Salad), 49; Israeli Couscous, 91; Provençal Chicken, 22; Shrimp with Olives and Feta, 54
Oranges: Beets with Orange, 60; Spanish-Style Pork, 161
Orzo: Avgolemono Soupa, 47

Pancetta: Gambas y Jamón, 163; Penne di Pistache, 38; Sherry Mushrooms with Pancetta, 156; Warm Mushroom Salad, 63
Panini: Medianoche, 139; Pulled Pork Sandwiches, 177
Pantry staples, 188–91
Pasta: Avgolemono Soupa, 47; Leftover Pasta Frittata, 37; Mac Daddy Mac 'n' Cheese, 183; Pasta Mollica, 35; Penne di Pistache, 38; Red Wine Pasta, 36
Peaches: Chilled Peach Soup, 72; Fruit Bathed in Watermelon, 58
Peanut butter: Palaver Chicken, 81; Peanut Soup, 74
Peanut sauce: Stir-Fried Pork and Vegetables with Satay Sauce, 129
Peanuts: Hot Tin Roof Sundae, 185
Pearl onions: Coquette au Vin, 21; Stifado, 50
Pears: Burgundy Poached Pears, 25; Green Beans with Pears and Bacon, 64
Peas: Crab Fried Rice, 124; Potato and Pea Samosas, 108; Pulao, 105
Pecans: Roasted Butternut Squash with Pecans, Dried Cherries, and Blue Cheese, 174
Pepitas: Pepita Pork, 162
Peppers, bell. *See* Bell peppers
Peppers, sweet: Pork Chops Étoufée, 179; Roadhouse Steak and Beer Chili, 172; Thai Green Curry with Chicken and Rice, 132
Pho: Fast Faux Pho, 116
Pie crusts: Potato and Pea Samosas, 108; Torta di Porri (Leek Tart), 34. *See also* Puff pastry
Pistachios: Penne di Pistache, 38
Polenta: Mamaliga (Romanian Polenta with Feta), 67
Pomegranates and pomegranate juice: Fesenjan (Chicken with Pomegranate-Walnut Sauce), 101; Muhammara, 95; Pomegranate and Cucumber Salad, 84
Pork: Banh Mi, 126; Bourbon BBQ Ribs, 181; Carnitas Quesadillas, 164; General Tsao Pork, 130; Margarita

Pork Chops, 166; Pepita Pork, 162; Pork Chops Étoufée, 179; Pork Tikka Masala, 114; Pulled Pork Sandwiches, 177; Spanish-Style Pork, 161; Stir-Fried Pork and Vegetables with Satay Sauce, 129; Tonkatsu, 131; Tropical Tenderloin, 147. *See also* Bacon; Ham; Pancetta; Proscuitto
Potatoes: Breakfast Taco Bar, 170; Chile and Crab Chowder, 171; Farm Skillet Frittata, 169; Cracked Potatoes with Rosemary, 31; Hot Potato Salad with Bacon Dressing, 61; Papas Aplastadas (Smashed Potatoes), 138; Potato and Cauliflower Bhaji, 106; Potato and Pea Samosas, 108; Potato-Fennel-Leek Soup with Smoky Cheese, 12; Potato Gratin with Goat Cheese, 18; Potato-Kale Minestra, 28; Roasted Corn and Chile Chowder, 153
Proscuitto: Gambas y Jamón, 163
Puff pastry: Tarte Flambée, 17
Pumpkin: Moroccan Sweet Potato and Squash Stew, 76

Quinoa: Stuffed Bell Peppers, 66

Raisins: Pulao, 105; Ruz Bil-loz wa Bil-Tamar (Rice with Almonds and Dates), 85
Raspberry preserves: Lightning Quick Almond Cake, 26
Ratatouille: South of France Halibut, 20
Red peppers: Htipiti, 45; Muhammara, 95; Portobella-Hummus Burgers, 52
Rice: Arroz Verde, 155; Cherry Rice Pilaf, 87; Crab Fried Rice, 124; Curry and Yogurt Lamb Chops, 113; Eggs Poached in Tomato Sauce, 98; Fesenjan (Chicken with Pomegranate-Walnut Sauce), 101; Jollof Rice, 78; Maui Beef on Coconut Rice with Macadamia Nuts and Basil, 144; Mujadara, 92; Palaver Chicken, 81; Pulao, 105; Ruz Bil-loz wa Bil-Tamar (Rice with Almonds and Dates), 85; Spicy Coconut Rice, 77; Tahdig, 86; Thai Green Curry with Chicken and Rice, 132
Rice noodles: Fast Faux Pho, 116
Rice sticks: General Tsao Pork, 130

Salad dressings: Hot Potato Salad with Bacon Dressing, 61; Salade Verte Vinaigrette, 14; Wasabi Slaw, 120
Salads: Black Bean Salad, 134; Carne Asada Salad, 154; Fattoush, 93; Green Beans with Pears and Bacon, 64; Horiatiki Salata (Greek Village Salad), 49; Hot Potato Salad with Bacon Dressing, 61; Laccha (Tomato and Cucumber Salad), 103; Mango-Lango Salad, 135; Pomegranate and Cucumber Salad, 84; Salade Verte, 14; Sicilian Lemon Salad, 30; Thai Beef Salad, 119; Warm Mushroom Salad, 63; Wasabi Slaw, 120
Salsa: Carne Asada Salad, 154; Frat Brats, 68; Grilled Swordfish with Mango Salsa, 137; Maque Choux Cakes, 176; Shrimp Cocktail with Salsa Verde, 159
Samosas: Potato and Pea Samosas, 108

ABOUT THE AUTHOR

© Yvette Sharis

Cherie Mercer Twohy is author of *The I Love Trader Joe's Cookbook* and *The I Love Trader Joe's Party Cookbook*. She teaches cooking at her school, Chez Cherie, in La Cañada, California (www.chezcherie.com). Her husband and three children have served as (mostly) enthusiastic recipe-testers, for which they have her eternal gratitude. Twohy holds a Certified Culinary Professional (CCP) designation from the International Association of Culinary Professionals, and a Level 1 Sommelier certificate from the Court of Master Sommeliers. Cherie can be reached at cherie@ilovetraderjoes.com.